This book is dedicated to the men, women, and children who have covered me with their prayers and whom I have covered with my prayers.

Mrs. Mary Dolores "Zulu" Lee Tyler Orphe
My Mother
October 11, 1930–September 5, 2005

Mr. Joseph "Joe Pete" John Orphe
My Father
December 13, 1925–October 4, 2010

Stella JoAnn Orphe Batiste
My Sister
March 3, 1958–October 15, 2005

Ruby George Orphe
My Sister-in-Law
February 14, 1955–April 9, 1995

Melissa Ann Orphe
My Niece
July 7, 1986–March 10, 2004

Tylan Mekel Janise Orphe
My Great-Niece
July 29, 1994–March 10, 2004

IN MEMORIAM

My adoptive church daughter, Dr. Keion Davis Parker, who died in 2020.

My Zeta Phi Beta Sorority, Incorporated, Alpha Gamma Zeta Chapter—New Orleans Sorority Sisters, Rev. Barbara Hamilton, Doris Pitts, and Jacquelyn and Lauren McMillians, who died in 2020.

The more than three hundred thousand people who lost their lives in 2020 because of COVID-19.

ACKNOWLEDGMENTS

I want to thank all who, over the years, have encouraged me to write a book.

I also want to thank the thirty-two contributors who took the time to send original prayers and personal poems to help us get through the year 2020.

Thank you to all who sent pictures of themselves, family members, and friends wearing a hat.

I am grateful to my family for allowing me to share their stories, which are part of my story, in this book.

I also want to express gratitude to Dr. Rosalind Pijeaux Hale, my Zeta Phi Beta Sorority, Inc., sorority sister and mentor, for her Zeta hat-wearing fundraiser that so inspired and encouraged me to write this book.

Special thank you to Ashley Orphe and Sharika Batiste Hawkins for putting the book together. I could not have done this work without them. This was a great family project. Your names should be on the front cover of this book.

I also want to thank friends and family who read the entire book or portions of this book and made suggestions and corrections. I thank Janet Harvey, Linda Perrodin Mallery, Sharika Batiste Hawkins, and Ashley Orphe.

I want to thank my dear friend Dr. Ouida Lee for referring me to AuthorHouse.

Thank you to my check-in coordinator, Raven Tan, and my publishing service associate, Vince Chappell, and the support team at AuthorHouse.

And last but not least, I want to thank God for the vision and the journey of writing this book. I have been able to tell this story, and may God get the glory. It has been a blessing for me, and I hope it blesses you, the reader.

PREFACE

Living through 2020: Covered by Prayers and Hats is a review of the year 2020 in a collection of original prayers and poems that helped us focus on God, encouraged us, and inspired us. My original concept was to gather prayers, poems, and pictures from others and place them in categories of love, healing, social justice, guidance, peace, fear, and hope. In conversations, people suggested that since the prayers and poems have stories behind them, I should tell of my relationship to the prayer, poem, or the person (author), thereby making the book a more exciting read. Again, this is a totally different concept and direction than what I thought I would be doing with this book. So here it is.

In looking back over the challenging events of the past year, I have joined my prayers and experiences with the prayers, poems, reflections, and pictures of thirty-two contributing friends, of which sixteen are pastors, and other friends and family, from three different countries, including England, Canada, and the United States.

We are from different backgrounds, but we were experiencing the same unprecedented events. Included are some short prayers, long prayers, general prayers of thanksgiving and praise for all days, and some prayers that relate directly to the challenging events we endured during the year—all from the heart. A friend suggested that since I like to quilt, I should quilt the pieces of these original independent prayers, poems, and photos of the book together. And so this is my attempt at quilting this review of 2020 together.

At the end of each chapter, you, the reader, are invited to reflect upon your 2020 year as you respond to this review. Your answers can remain as entries in your own personal prayer journal or can serve as discussion topics in a group.

May this quilt of inspirational and encouraging prayers, poems, and pictures remind us that living through 2020 during the global COVID-19 pandemic and in the midst of racial divide and social unrest in the United States, we were indeed covered by prayer!

CHAPTER 1

Somebody prayed for me

For me, "covered by prayers" is the concept of "I pray for you; you pray for me. We pray for others, and others pray for us." We stand in the prayer gap for others. We pray to God. We talk with God. We make our petitions known to God. We know the power of prayer, the power of talking to God.

Praying also means we listen to God when God speaks to us. We are communicating with God, and God is communicating with us. We can talk with God for ourselves, and others can talk to God for us. That is covering us in prayer. As the old gospel song entitled "Somebody prayed for me" says,

> Somebody prayed for me, they had me on their mind.
> They took the time and prayed for me.
> I'm so glad they prayed.
> I'm so glad they prayed for me.
> I'm so glad they prayed.
> I'm so glad they prayed for me.[1]

The song indicates that others pray for us. My momma prayed for me. My daddy prayed for me. My sister prayed for me. My brother prayed for me. The church prayed for me. The preacher prayed for me. We are grateful and glad that people prayed for us. They took their time and covered us by prayers.

---

[1]   1. Dorothy Norwood, "Somebody Prayed for Me," on *Live with the Georgia Mass Choir*, MALACO, 1994, compact disc.

Dolores "Zulu" Orphe and Joseph "Joe Pete" Orphe

Martha Orphe, father, Joseph Orphe, and mother, Dolores Orphe

I am glad and grateful that I am the product of a praying mother, father, family, friends, and church. My parents are Joseph John Orphe and Mary Dolores Lee Tyler Orphe. There are five children from their union and one stepdaughter: Phyllis Tyler Anthony Linzer, Clara Tyler Jean Batiste, Wilbert John Orphe, Stella JoAnn Orphe Batiste, Martha Marie Orphe, and Loucinda "Cindy" Marie George.

Joseph and Dolores Orphe family
Standing from left to right: Stella Orphe Batiste, Martha Orphe, Phyllis Tyler Anthony Linzer, Wilbert Orphe, Clara Tyler Jean Batiste, Loucinda George
Seated: Dolores Orphe and Joseph Orphe
Mother's seventy-fourth birthday party, October 2004

We were raised in beautiful St. Martinville, Louisiana, located in the Acadiana area in the center of the state. Dad was an okra farmer. The five children and our parents picked the okra. Mom also worked in a pepper factory, and Dad was also a road construction worker. Our parents did everything in their earthly power to provide for the family, but they knew we needed the help of the Lord to survive living in Jim Crow Louisiana.

Our mother died September 4, 2005, a week after Hurricane Katrina landed in the center and eastern New Orleans area of the state. Upon her death, I saw in her Bible where she had written our names near Bible verses. One of the ways my mother prayed for her children was by praying specific Bible verses for each child and our families.

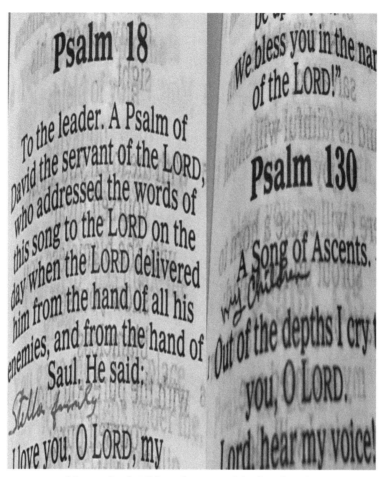
My mother's Bible—she prayed for her family.

For example, in the book of Psalms, we appear in the following order:

Psalm 18—Stella's family
Psalm 20—Phyllis's family
Psalm 25—Wilbert "Cabay" and Ruby's family
Psalm 27—Dolores and Joseph's children
Psalm 31—Ruby and Cabay's family
Psalm 40—Dolores and Joseph's children
Psalm 42—Dolores
Psalm 46—Dolores
Psalm 73—Dolores
Psalm 118—Dolores and Joseph's children
Psalm 121—Dolores and Ruby
Psalm 128—Cabay and Ruby
Psalm 130—My children
Psalm 131—Clara
Psalm 138—Martha
Psalm 143—Martha
Psalm 149—Dolores
Psalm 150—Dolores

I was glad to see that our mother covered us, our father, and herself in prayer.

Our family covered one another in our prayers. Of all the siblings, Stella was our prayer warrior. We know she prayed for us and so many others. Our phenomenal woman of God died October 15, 2005, only a month and a half after our mother died and three weeks after Hurricane Rita landed in the center and western Lake Charles area of Louisiana.

We were caught in the middle of two hurricanes within two months. We experienced so much devastation and loss in such a short period of time: two hurricanes and two praying matriarchs. We believe Stella and our mother, our prayer giants, are watching over us and praying for us even now from heaven.

Phyllis Tyler Anthony Linzer family
Left to right: Billy, Carlus, Shyla, Jardell, LaKrisha, Jacolby, Jakaylon, Jterira, Keisha, Japerra, Marvin, Raquan, Racheal, Horace, Horacio, Phyllis, Damon, Kera
Dolores Orphe's seventy-fourth birthday celebration, October 2004

Phyllis Tyler Anthony Linzer family
Jardell, Jakaylon, Shyla, Carlus, LaKrisha, Rachael, Japerra, Keisha, Kera, Janavian, and John
July 2020

Clara Tyler Jean Batiste family
Monica, Murphy, Clara, Keyvon, Steve, Kayvon, LaKaysha, Dolores, Joseph
October 2004

Kayvon, Stephen "Steve," LaKeya, Monica, LaKaysha, Keyvon
2019

Wilbert "Cabay" Orphe family
Standing: Tisha, Ashley
Seated: Wilbert, Ruby, Kizzie, Melissa

Standing: Ashley, Jackie, Kizzie
Babies: Jaylen and Jayden, Wilbert, Tisha
Seated: Dolores, Joseph
October 2004

Stella JoAnn Orphe Batiste family
Standing: Shawntae, Stella, William, Sharika
Seated: Dolores, Joseph
October 2004

Shawntae Batiste, William Batiste, Sharika Batiste Hawkins, Jerry Hawkins Jr.
2018

Martha Orphe family
Dolores, Martha, Joseph
2004

Martha Orphe
Christopher Follins and Sheradi Jackson Follins
2019

Orphe siblings
Phyllis, Clara, Martha, Cindy, and Wilbert
January 2021

Some of our family gathered for worship at Mallalieu United Methodist Church.
February 2018

I was blessed to be raised by a church that prayed and continues to pray for me. Mallalieu United Methodist Church in St. Martinville prayed for me while I was in the womb. Women such as Momma Moss, Cousin Violetta Charles, Mrs. Florita Johnson, Mrs. Antonia George, Cousin Victoria James, Cousin Hilda, Theta Compton, and Emily Orphe McCoy were just a few of the many church members who prayed for me and helped me during my childhood. Rev. Babin, Rev. Wesley, and Rev. Raymond also covered me with their prayers as preachers.

Top photo: "Momma" Patsy Moss, Emily McCoy
Bottom photo: Communion stewards:
Violetta Charles, Florita Johnson, Antonia George, Victoria James
Mallalieu UMC members

Top photo, seated, Cousin Hilda Alexander
Lower photo: Rev. Raymond, Theta Compton
Mallalieu UMC

They prayed for me as a little Black girl growing up with a speech impediment so damaging that I could not pronounce the *d, th,* and *s* sounds. I looked and sounded different from the other children, but the church loved me. The church loved me and told me that Jesus also loved me. The church encouraged me to do my best, be my best, and give God my best. Even with my speech difficulties, I was encouraged to read scriptures and recite poems to the congregation just like the other children. They would call out to me and say, "Take your time, baby! You can do it." It might have taken me some time, but I did it. I did my best. And I would receive big hugs. Oh, how I loved those hugs!

I remember well Momma Moss laying my head in her large bosom and thinking, *This must be what being in the shelter of God is like as described in Psalm 91.* I loved God and I loved to go to church, where I felt warm, safe, and protected from what I often experienced as people being hurtful, mean, and ugly to me because of my speech. The Mallalieu ladies would not allow anybody to even think they could tease me and hurt me. I believe it was the love of the God that I felt at the church.

The church encouraged me to be my best. I was my best at the segregated Adam Carlson Elementary School. I was an active straight-A student. Like the women at church, the teachers took time with me and taught me how to speak as clearly as possible.

I wish I had a picture of me during those years, but I do not. Our family lost a lot of pictures over the years. I never had a full set of adult teeth; in fact, I only had twelve. In 2007, I learned that I had a medical condition called *hypodontia*, which is a lack of sufficient bone mass to support adult teeth development. Not having a medical understanding of what happened to me did not prevent some people in the town and even cousins from calling me names, like "monkey," "monster," "old black bull," "butt-ugly," just to name a few. In school, some of the girls would chase me away because they did not want to play with me, or if they allowed me to play, I had to be the bull that chased them. Sometimes, I would tell my beautiful sister Stella, and she would handle the matter. I focused on doing my best at my schoolwork.

When the public schools in my town integrated in the 1960s, the new powers that be decided that because I could not speak English, as they referred to my speech difficulties, they would place me in what was then called the "mentally retarded" class. That's what was communicated to my parents, although no diagnostic tests were used to reach that conclusion. It was erroneously believed that I had not done nor could I do any schoolwork. As time went on, disproportionately more Black students with "behavioral problems," such as cutting school or fighting, were placed in that class with me. The hallmark of those types of classes was no curriculum, no teaching, and little supervision. I remember having to fight off the sexual advances of the older boys.

My school world had turned upside down. That classification heightened the hurt and pain for me. People teased me and laughed at me. I was now seen not only as ugly but as an ugly, *dumb* Black girl. How could I be a straight-A student one day and the next be labeled "mentally retarded"? In hindsight, I can see that this adversity made me stronger, and now I fight for people diagnosed with what is called "intellectual disability" (ID) because someone prayed and fought for me.

My parents and church members, especially Mrs. Emily McCoy, fought for me and prayed for me. Sadly, it took longer to remove me from that setting than it took to reach the arbitrary decision to put me in it and mislabel me. So many other Black students were treated unfairly as I was.

Thankfully, we were able to address our concerns for me, and thus in the sixth grade, I had dental work done and was placed in speech therapy. Over the years, I struggled with my speech. I was teased with "Bet you can't say that again" and called names like "Slippy Slupper" and "Cicely Tyson's Old Jane Pittman." I would tell my big brother Wilbert what they said. If needed, he would fight those who teased me. He would protect me. The Cicely Tyson comment was meant to be derogatory, but for me, it was a compliment. Cicely Tyson was a beautiful, strong Black woman, and I decided I wanted to be just like her and like my momma, who was a force to be reckoned with.

I began to show some progress with my speech therapy. I became active in school and some of the local Black churches in town. I had accepted Jesus as my personal Lord and Savior and continued to experience his love. I loved Jesus and I loved going to church. Some Sundays, I would attend the 7:00 a.m. Notre Dame Catholic Church worship service, where my sister Stella and I were active in the youth group. Then I went to the 8:30 a.m. Mallalieu United Methodist Church worship service. And then I attended the Union Baptist Church worship service. I was appreciative of the support I received as a young Christian Youth.

I asked my parents to allow me to convert to Catholicism so that I could become a cloistered nun. They said yes, but the summer I was to visit the convent, my mother sent me to Denver, Colorado. Little did she or I know, I would meet a woman minister! To all our surprise, even with speech therapy, at the age of fifteen, I received and said yes to God's call upon my life to be a preacher.

When I told Mallalieu Church, they were excited. Momma Moss placed my head in her large bosom and told me she was not surprised; she knew all the time because she had been praying for me. They continued to pray for me. I continued with speech therapy until I graduated with honors from St. Martinville Senior School. I said the prayer at my graduation.

Mallalieu Church helped me and so many others to overcome obstacles in life. They forged in us the power of prayer to God, family, hard work, and determination. They covered me and others in prayer. Throughout this book, I will identify some of my friends who prayed and continue to pray for me. I am so glad they prayed for me.

Since childhood, I have learned the power of being covered in prayer and the power of others praying for me. As an adult, not as a cloistered nun but as an ordained United Methodist Minister, I continue to know and live in the power of being covered in prayer. Prayer and praying for others is in my DNA. Prayer was my saving grace.

I was raised in the prayer tradition and also in the hat-wearing tradition. Prayers covered us, and for me, hats are an outward manifestation of that protection. When I was growing up in the 1960s and 1970s, women knew how to wear their beautiful hats at Mallalieu United Methodist Church. My mother, one of the most beautiful, strongest women I have ever known, knew how to wear a hat. Most of the women worked a long, hard week, but come Sunday morning, they dressed up with their hats. They were beautiful and confident and gave God their best. Growing up as a child being called ugly, I saw true beauty in that church.

At the age of seventeen, I left home to attend Centenary College of Louisiana in Shreveport, Louisiana. Some forty years later, I permanently returned to my birthplace. As I traveled the world in my younger years, I found ways to keep myself connected to God, to my family, to my culture. For example, my mother, sister Stella, and I read *The Upper Room Daily Devotional*. It kept us connected to each other and to God.

When I moved to Pittsburgh, where I lived for twenty-one years, I missed some of my Southern traditions, food, worship style, and so on. I had changed location in life, but I still felt a need to connect to my familiar. I wore hats as a way of remembering how God protected me and was with me. I wore hats also as my way of remembering my family and where I came from. My hats kept me connected. My hats helped me feel those warm, safe, protected, and covered feelings I felt when I was a child in church. Over the years, those hats became who I am. I am a hat wearer. I have been wearing them my entire adult life.

Today, in so many churches, hat wearing is a dying tradition. I enjoy dressing up for God and giving God my best. I love hats! I own over one hundred! When I wear a hat, it connects me to those who covered me in the past. Wearing a hat grounds and reminds me of how I was formed in the crucible of the Black Methodist church. Like my mother and others, I feel very confident and beautiful when I wear my hats.

Hatitude

I have "hattitude" when I wear my hats. If I am blessed with longevity, I would like to carry off wearing a hat like Cicely Tyson wore at Aretha Franklin's funeral in 2018.

Cicely Tyson: Aretha Franklin's Funeral 2018
Cicely Tyson – 96 years old
December 19, 1924—January 28, 2021

Purchased hat at Hattitude Hat Shop, Martha's Vineyard, wore hat all over the world
Upper right picture: Trip to London and Paris
Lower photos: The Kennedy Center, Washington, DC

For over thirty years as a pastor in the ministry, I looked forward to wearing a hat on the Sundays when I did not preach. In some of the churches I pastored, I was teased that I was the pastor and the first lady. I intentionally did not include any pictures (in this book) of the hat-wearing ladies from the churches I served, but I want to recognize those churches: Smithfield United Church, the Community of Reconciliation Church, and Albright United Methodist Church, all in Pittsburgh, Pennsylvania, and First Street Peck Wesley United Methodist Church and Williams Ross United Methodist Church, both in New Orleans, Louisiana.

If I, an ordained United Methodist Pastor, an elder, had not already decided to be buried in my clergy robe, I probably would want to be buried in one of my hats. Hat wearing may be a dying tradition for some people but not for me. I will wear a hat at any occasion but especially funerals and weddings. Sometimes I am the only person wearing a hat at an event. I enjoy the conversations that are started because of my hats.

At her mother's funeral in Toronto, Canada, Rev. Eleanor Scarlett's young niece Shannae told me she liked the hat I was wearing. She asked if she could have it. I told her she could have all my hats when I died. She asked me, "When you gonna die?" Shannae is now twenty-five years old. I don't know if she or anybody will really want my hats when I die, but I want them while I am living.

Hats are just that much a part of my life. Hat wearing is who I am. And I thank God. I feel covered by prayers and covered by hats. Thus the title of this book, *Living through 2020: Covered by Prayers and Hats.*

Reflection

Reflections on Prayer
by
Rev. Clifton Conrad Sr.

Good morning beloved!

When you think about the most important elements or properties in the life of a believer, one of the things that come to my mind is prayer. Prayer is essential to all that we say and do as a believer. It is the essence of who we are.

Through prayer, we are invited into the presence of the Lord. Prayer is our lifeline which we throw out and pull ourselves toward God. Prayer is not a once a day monologue, with us doing the talking, that we have with God. It is an ongoing conversation that flavors and tempers our day. It is always a good time to pray! (Read 2 Chronicles 7:14)

Gracious God, You have provided the line of communication, which we call prayer. Lord, we accept Your invitation to enter into Your presence and to be in conversation with You. We thank you for Your open ears hear each and every word that comes from our lips. We thank You for each prayer answered, as we go about our journey today. *In the name of Jesus we pray. Amen.*

***

Rev. Clifton Conrad and I have served on various committees and in various organizations throughout the Louisiana Conference of the United Methodist Church and the state of Louisiana. We are both colleagues and friends. Rev. Clifton Conrad is the senior pastor at Asbury and St. Matthew Churches on the New Orleans West Bank. He writes a daily reflection/devotion on Facebook. He originally sent them only to his family. Then he started sharing them with his churches. He then posted them on Facebook so even more people could read them. These reflections became part of my daily devotions. They helped me and so many others weather the storms of the difficult 2020 year.

You are invited to read his daily Facebook devotionals at the following link: https://www.facebook.com/clifton.sr.1

I offer end-of-the-chapter journal reflections because during the writing of this book, I was brought to an old painful place in my life. I felt the hurt in telling my speech impediment story. I cried. I needed a moment, and I prayed. I talked to God. I hope these reflection moments give you, the reader, an opportunity to reflect and talk to God. Pray.

Reflections: Chapter 1

Covered by prayers—"I pray for you; you pray for me."

1. Who are some of the people you pray for?

2. Somebody prayed for me. Who are some of the people who are praying for you?

3. It is always a good time to pray. Accept your invitation to enter into the presence of God and be in conversation with Him. Pray some prayers. Write a short one here to share with your group if you so desire:

Read 2 Chronicles 7:14.

Follow Rev. Conrad's daily devotionals at the following link:

https://www.facebook.com/clifton.sr1

Hat and pearls

CHAPTER 2

We prayed

Most of us would agree that the year 2020 started out like any other year. Many of us woke up each morning and said our prayers. We prayed for our families, friends, churches, and communities. We were covered by prayer, and we covered others in prayer.

Prayer

Joseph Family's Daily Prayer
by
Wanda and Neva Joseph

This prayer starts our day. We, Patrick, Wanda, and Neva, developed it to cover the bases for the cares we determined were crucial to our success: spiritually, physically, socially, mentally, and beyond.

Lord bless our going out and our coming in. Cover us in your darling son Jesus Christ's blood. Order our footsteps in the ways that they should go. Forgive us all of our sins, everything we've done, said and thought wrong, knowingly and unknowingly and love our souls freely once again—as we forgive those who have trespassed against us. Give us safe traveling grace as we go to and fro. If one of us, some of us, or all of us should face death or the rapture, we ask to be made worthy to enter into your kingdom where we'll praise your name forevermore. If not, let us make it home safely where we'll be a family again. This we ask in Jesus Christ's name, Amen.

Wanda Joseph, Rev. Martha, Neva Joseph
My worship team First Street Peck Wesley United Methodist Church, New Orleans, LA

***

Wanda Joseph (on the left) and I are spiritual sisters and mothers. Neva Joseph, my adoptive daughter, was my church music director. Neva and her choir member and mother, Wanda, helped me to worship and to lead worship at First Street Peck Wesley United Methodist Church, New Orleans, Louisiana. Many times, as pastors, it is difficult to both worship and lead worship. I thank God that they, along with others, covered me in prayers that allowed the Spirit of God to move in mighty ways.

Poem

Our Family
by
Mrs. Charity (Turp) Turpeau, MEd

Our family members are God's gift from above,
We stick together with laughs, prayers, and love.

We listen to understand and never demand,
and never alone will any of our family stand.

Our family is forgiving and has patience during each other's race.
It's humbling to witness God's love and continuous grace.

Our family is happy, blessed, and even quite the same
for example: never turning their back or quick to place blame.

If your family is not like this, its ok and don't be sad
Because this isn't just my family, it's **Our Family** so now be glad.

***

Charity is my second cousin. Her name is just who she is—giving. When she can, she helps us as a family to bless others. Charity is a creative sixth-grade math educator at Acadian Middle School in Lafayette, Louisiana, where she was named 2020–2021 Teacher of the Year!

Prayer

Morning Prayer
by
Rev. Dr. Jennie Curry

Father, in the name of Jesus, I thank you for watching over me all night long as I slept in peace, joy and happiness and for waking me up with your alarm clock. Thank you for the revelation of your word and presence in my heart and spirit. I thank you for the forgiveness of sin and any unrighteousness. I forgive anyone who has committed a trespass against me with mercy.

Father I thank you for redeeming me from the curse of poverty and lack and as I walk in victory spiritually, physically, socially, financially and academically.

Thank you that I am who your words say I am, the righteous of God, a joint-heir of Jesus, a world-overcomer and more than a conqueror and I can do all things through Christ who strengthens me.

***

Rev. Dr. Jennie L. Curry and I enjoy our clergywoman sisterhood. We also enjoy being sorority sisters. Rev. Curry is the pastor of Morris Brown African Methodist Episcopal (AME) Church, New Orleans, Louisiana.

Prayer

Grace of God
Submitted by Sonya Pierre

The Grace of God in my life shall perplex my enemies and problems in the name of Jesus!

***

Sonya indicated, "This prayer was given to me to pray in 2016 by my sister in Christ Donna Faye Batiste Clement, who became my big sister after Stella JoAnn Orphe Batiste, my sister in Christ, died. She gave me this when I was struggling with my MS diagnosis, symptoms, and acceptance of it! To God be the glory!"

Testimony Tuesday

I had an exam today and was asked by another patient what happened to me? I told her I was diagnosed with MS years ago. She responded, I am sorry. I told her no need to be sorry.

Mrs. Sonya Johnson Pierre
Mallalieu Church member

***

Sonya and I are spiritual sisters and church members who worship together at Mallalieu UMC in St. Martinville, Louisiana.

Prayer

A Prayer of Praise
by
Rev. Eleanor Mackey Cushenberry, ThD

O God, Awesome and Almighty,
We praise you just for who you are!
We praise You, O God, for Your Love that is beyond our deserving.
We praise You, O God, for Your Peace that goes beyond our understanding.
We praise You, O God, for Your Leading that shelters us on the right path.
We praise You! O God!
For all You have done,
For all You are doing,
For all You will do.
We love You, O God
only because You first loved us.
Now, O God,
Have Your own way.
Melt us.
Mold us.
Fill us.
Use us.
For Your Glory alone. AMEN!

***

Rev. Eleanor Cushenberry, ThD, is a powerful praying pastor and friend. We have supported each other as women of God in ministry in Louisiana. She is the shepherd of God's flock at Camphor United Methodist Church in Baton Rouge, Louisiana.

Prayer

A Prayer of Thanksgiving
by
Janet Harvey

My Father in Heaven, I come to you this time with praise and understanding.

I praise your Holy Name. I thank you for your unconditional love. I thank you for never ceasing to care for, and guide this sometimes disobedient child.

As I come to you today Heavenly Father, I am most grateful for you allowing and encouraging me to call you Father! I am most grateful for your love for me, that you still call me your child. That knowledge is like a warm blanket to me.

Dear God I have come to know, and appreciate what it means to call you "Heavenly FATHER". You have cared for me when I didn't deserve it. You have cared for me even when I disobeyed you! You did not desert me, and I thank you dear Father. You have cared for me when I was obedient, and revealed even more to me. Thank you for allowing me to call you, My Father!

My Father in Heaven, I thank you for these quiet times when I can come to you and confess my sins, my disobedience, my shortcomings, and my willfulness. I thank you for never losing faith in your child!

Dear Father in Heaven, I thank you with all my heart, with all my soul, with all my might, and all my body. I beg you to continue your work on me. I thank you for your love. I thank you for your trust in me—having the ability to walk in your path.

My Father in Heaven, this is my prayer of thanksgiving. I thank you for our quiet time together. I love you my Father.

AMEN, AMEN, AND AMEN!

**

Jan and I are blessed to be members of Mallalieu United Methodist Church. Both of us were and are covered by the prayers of the church members. We both left home and have since returned. We are sisters in Christ as we pray, worship, and serve God together. Jan Harvey worked for Amtrak for thirty-four years as manager of passenger services training and manager of employee services, and she retired as manager of stations, managing the operations of four states.

So in early 2020, I did the same as everybody else. I woke up and said my prayers. I too was grateful for the quiet time with God. I too prayed for my family. I prayed prayers of praise and thanksgiving. I was grateful for the grace of God and knowing that I am more than a conqueror. And I went to church to worship God together with others. As a person living with disabilities, under a doctor's care, on twenty-four/seven oxygen, thankful to be alive, I was trying to live every day to its fullest with the help of family and friends.

I have several items on my bucket list to accomplish before I die. So I started 2020 with much gusto. In January, I traveled with all my medical equipment and supplies with three family members to New York City for the Martin Luther King Jr. holiday. In February, my family had nearly seventy-five people at my house for the Super Bowl in the 1,500-square-foot family room. Also in February, I went with two friends to the Rotary Club Mardi Gras Ball in St. Martinville, Louisiana, and then I went with three family members to the Zulu Mardi Gras Ball (in a ball gown riding on my electric scooter) in New Orleans, Louisiana.

Mardi Gras, New Orleans
February 2020

We continued to pray. And life continued. At the beginning of March, some family members and friends formed the Orphe Generational Foundation, a Christian-based 501(c)3 organization created to impact the lives of people across the generations in the community through scholarship, education, and community service. The launch and initial community service event was a "Blessing Boutique" in which the foundation would bless others by giving gently worn or new clothes and other items to the community. The event was scheduled for Saturday, March 21, and Sunday, March 22. But as the days of mid-March were passing, we found ourselves canceling the event and instead focusing our attention on buying up all the masks, gloves, toilet paper, hand sanitizer, disinfect cleaners, and bleach that we could find. And we prayed.

Reflections: Chapter 2

1. What spoke to you from the prayers, poems, and photos?

2. Write a prayer of praise and thanksgiving:

3. Where were you in March 2020?

Physically?

Emotionally?

Spiritually?

Today's Date:

Where are you today

Physically?

Emotionally?

Spiritually?

We never know what the future will hold ...

CHAPTER 3

COVID-19 Pandemic

By late March, *everything stopped*, was cancelled, or was postponed. We were in a global health pandemic with the killer coronavirus, also known as COVID-19. It was disturbing to many of us in the United States that leaders in the federal government knew of the threat and danger of this disease as early as January, if not earlier. Some leaders wanted to address the forming crisis, while others called it a hoax. Many of us had already traveled and gathered in large groups. Sadly, I knew people who attended both the Mardi Gras balls I had just attended in February and caught COVID-19. Some of them died from it. We did not know. We were not told about the virus. The virus was spreading, and people were dying.

We were under the stay-at-home order to stop the spread of the virus. We sheltered at home, quarantined, day after day, not knowing when we would be allowed to go out.

Prayer

Waking Up Every Sunday
by
Elsa Boler
London, England

Me and my dad wake up every Sunday ready to go to church
The sun shines the birds sing
When we walk down the Aisle to take our seat
Every one smiled at us
I felt so welcome
When the prayers finished
They called out all the children to go to Sunday school
As all the children gathered
The chatter started
And the laughs started
But now we can't do that anymore
The clouds turned grey
The world turned grey
Because of a deadly virus ...

Elsa Boler, London, England

***

Eleven-year-old Elsa Camille Boler lives with her parents, William "Billy" and Esther Boler, in London, England (South London). Before the lockdowns, she attended Tooting Methodist Church, where she participated in the 2019 Children's Christmas church play, but it was canceled in 2020 because of the virus. Elsa enjoys gymnastics, dance, soccer, and music.

Ruth G. Richard with grandbaby Elsa Boler

Elsa is the beloved granddaughter of my lifetime wise friend and mentor Ruth G. Richardson. Ruth was of the Bhai faith. When my soul was disturbed and distressed, Ruth would ask me, "What did your Big Man up there say?" I could count on Ruth to lead me to God for guidance and to cover me with her prayers. Ruth was a retired social worker and former executive director of Three Rivers Youth in Pittsburgh and a noted artist. I watched Ruth pour life, love, and knowledge into her granddaughter Elsa, as she did with me.

Ruth G. Richardson
March 30, 1926–June 9, 2019

Prayer

What Do I Do When …?
by
Rev. John Winn

Dear God,
What do I do when my fragile words are inadequate
for the freight of meaning I seek?
What do I do when my prayer has no voice, no substance,
only sighs and groans and silence?
What do I do when the "earthquake, wind, and fire,"
shake and sway and burn me deep within?
What do I do when the "still, small, voice"
is subdued by the loudness all around?
What do I do when there is no epiphany, no "Aha"?
I know, Dear God, I know,
you have prepared me well:
I remind myself of the truest thing I know.
I let faith take me where facts can never go.
I seek someone whose warm embrace rekindles my life.
I return to that quiet place within
where I have found answers before.

Then, I wait;
actively wait.
Thank you for meeting me there.
Amen.

John Winn, *For All Seasons* (Preachers' Aid Society of New England, 2011)

***

Rev. John Winn is a retired elder in the Louisiana Conference of the United Methodist Church. He is a respected leader, mentor, and friend among the pastors and laity of the conference. He is also a writer. He is my gifted friend in the ministry.

Rev. Carol Cotton Winn, colleagues in the ministry

Rev. Carol Cotton Winn is a retired elder in the Louisiana Conference of the United Methodist Church. She is my pastoral friend and colleague in the ministry. Rev. Carol and Rev. John are the parents of Rev. Callie Winn Crawford, who also is a retired elder. She is a good friend to me.

Julian wearing her grandfather's hat

Rev. Callie sketched the drawing of her niece Julian, who is the granddaughter of Rev. Carol and Rev. John. We did not plan this, but Julian is wearing her grandfather John's hat. They are covering her in prayers and hats.

Prayer
Category: Guidance

Guide Us Each Day
by
Rev. Dr. Tara Sutton

Divine Waymaker,

Guide our footsteps as we journey through mountaintop and valley experiences. Walk with us each day and be our guiding light. You are our Way Maker who orders our steps in you. Strengthen and counsel us through troubling times to bring us to a place of peace. Direct our days to bring glory to your name and let us praise you for everything you have provided for us.

In Jesus' Name, Amen

Prayer
Category: Healing

Healing for Our Souls
by
Rev. Dr. Tara Sutton
Pastor Michigan Conference

Awesome Healer,

Allow your healing presence to completely heal every area in our lives. Restore our health in spiritual and physical bodies as you release any pain, discomfort and weariness we may be experiencing. Help us to trust in your divine timing to mend what is broken inside of us. Sometimes our spiritual healing will take precedence in our lives. So, undergird us as we let go of all our anxieties and repair the areas of brokenness, for we trust in you. In Jesus' Name, Amen

***

Rev. Tara has been the "sweet anointing prayer leader" for many of the Black clergywomen of the United Methodist Church (BCWUMC). I have experienced Rev. Tara's prayer rooms at the BCWUMC conferences as the place to go to be in the shelter of the wings of God and return to the ministry context, knowing that you have been in prayer.

Poem

Reflection
by
Linda Perrodin Mallery

We spend so much time moving and doing
And doing and moving
STOP!!!
Who did you help today?
Were you kind to your neighbor?

***

Linda Mallery and I have been friends for what seems like a lifetime. At our births in September 1959, Linda (September 29) and I (September 3) and our friend Rosalind James Griffin (September 12) were probably all in the same hospital at the same time and taken for our checkups and shots at the same time. We have been together ever since. Whether we talked or not, the three of us could pick up in each other's lives. Linda is a retired auditor. She received her bachelor of science in mechanical engineering from the University of Louisiana at Lafayette and her MBA from the University of Houston. She loves reading, working out, and spending time with family and friends. I am blessed to have Linda and Rosalind as my forever friends.

Prayer

Bidding Prayer
March 15, 2020
by
Rev. William Meekins

Please respond after each petition Lord in Your mercy hear our prayer ...

Let us pray ...

God we acknowledge that you are the God of all creation. We know that you are the source of our strength and the provider of our wisdom. We pray that in the morning and in the evening we will continue to praise your most holy name because of who you are.

Lord in Your mercy hear our prayer.

God we pray for the church universal, that we might find ways to work together, to affirm the humanity of each person, to seek justice for all of God's people regardless of location or station in life. As different Faith communities help us to have welcoming and willing spirits to offer hospitality, where your love shines forth. Help us to admit to our human failures, admitting our inabilities to live as one.

Lord in Your mercy hear our prayer.

In this season of Lent we are called to the reading of scripture in public and in private, a call to self-denial and self-reflection, and to live the gift of walking humbly before you. **Forgive us when our words and actions are filled with arrogance. Help when our spiritual walks are not reflective of who you are.**

Lord in Your Mercy hear our prayer.

We pray for each nation, for each community, each family and individuals impacted by the coronavirus. Help us to do our part to contain the spread of this disease, by washing our hands, by wearing face-coverings, by staying home when we are sick, by following the guidelines as recommended by health officials,

Lord in your mercy hear our prayer

We pray for our Mckeesport Shared ministry, our six campuses Beulah Park, Calvary, Christy Park, First, Kephart, and Wesley. We pray that we might live into the vision and the plans that you have given to us. That you might help us to walk with 20/20 vision not fearful of the future. Help us to trust that you have plans for us, plan not harm but plans to prosper us, plans for a future and hope. (Jeremiah 29:11)

Lord in Your mercy hear our prayer.

Lord we pray for those within our community, for those who are sick, those who are filled with anxiety, those who find it a challenge to care for loved ones, the addicted and those in-prisoned. We pray for those who you mention in the quietness of our hearts and minds.

Lord in your mercy hear our prayer …

We pray for our national elected political leaders, who are charged with working together to enact legislation that benefits all citizens and not for a select few. We pray for our state and local leaders. (use their names if possible or position) We pray that you will continue to provide them with the tools that are needed to govern effectively.

Lord in Your mercy hear our prayer

We pray for our general superintendent Cynthia Moore-Koiko and our superintendent Patricia A. Nelson.

Lord in your mercy hear our prayer

Lord we pray in silence for the unspoken needs for those individual needs that run so deep within our spirits...

Silence

Lord we pray this in the name of the One who taught us how to pray ...

***

Rev. William B. Meekins Jr. and I have been friends for over forty years and have served in ministry together for twenty years. Rev. William is an elder in the Western Pennsylvania Conference of the United Methodist Church. He serves as the senior pastor of the McKeesport Shared Ministry, which is composed of six campuses: Beulah Park, Calvary, Christy Park, First, Kephart, and Wesley.

Prayer
May 5, 2020, Wednesday, 12:15 p.m.

From Struggles to Strength
by
Rev. Dr. Orphe

I would like to thank my Zeta Phi Beta Sorority, Incorporated, Alpha Gamma Zeta Chapter New Orleans, president, Mary Carter, for the inspiring speech she delivered on May 4, 2020, to her students at West Jefferson High School in New Orleans, Louisiana. That speech inspired this prayer as we remember our struggles will make us stronger when we go from struggles to strength.

Let us pray.

Lord, **as a world, we are struggling as we are fighting the COVID-19 virus of Pandemic size**. We are praying for an end to this virus and its deadly results. Remind us dear Lord that you have Power over death and that even in our struggles, our fight with **this disease that has weakened the whole wide world, we can be strong, we can become stronger and we will as a world be stronger again.**

Lord Jesus as a country we in the United States are struggling, not only as we are facing a deadly disease which has taken the lives of thousands upon thousands of people, but **as a country we are struggling to find our way—Morally, Economically, Emotionally.**

Lord, we are struggling looking for leadership that would give us steady, healthy ways to protect all the people of the nation and restart our economy. Remind us, O Lord, of the many times the people of Israel in the Old Testament of the Holy Bible wanted to trust in man rather than trust in you God. Help us in our struggle to seek you as God, our Sovereign and our King, and know that you have won over misguided nations in the past. We can win, if we put our full and unwavering trust in you. **We can be strong and we can be stronger and we will be stronger again.** The Bible reminds us, the name of the Lord is our strong tower.

Lord, **the State of Louisiana, like so many other states**, is struggling to lower our numbers of deaths and we are struggling to recover and become ourselves again, our love to enjoy life, party over here state again. Help us O Lord as we like others struggle to follow our stay at home order, as we struggle to determine when to go out, as we struggle with our safety and boredom. **Lord remind us that it's not just about me as an individual but we as a state**, a state full of elderly people, immune compromised people, virus carrying people, healthy men, women and children but that even as we are struggling remind us Lord, Jesus that you died for all of us that we might have life abundantly, healthy strong lives although weakened right now, but we can be strong, we can become stronger, we will be stronger again.

Lord, we **pray especially for our 2020 Graduates** all over this country. They and their families are struggling with how this could be happening to them, why, and why now!!

They have not been with school friends, church friends, community friends to do what others have been able to do in the past. They, and we their families, **are heartbroken and ever so disappointed** that they did not have proms, and award ceremonies and graduations at so many levels. They are struggling but help us help them to also know that these struggles will make them strong, they will become stronger as they tell their very different stories.

Help us O Lord we are struggling. *Help us to find strength in you and in each other, for you O lord our God, you are our refuge and our strength. Amen and Amen.*

COVID-19 was changing how we were living. We were in our homes. Some people had never spent so much time in our homes. What do we do at home? In the beginning, it felt good to do some back-burner projects. I started a quilt project. But as a country, we were struggling. Businesses were trying to determine how long they could be closed before they would be closed permanently. How do we live if the businesses are closed? Some companies turned their operations into the best technological configuration for the company to be able to continue. They provided for staff to work from home, provided internet services if needed. They provided laptop computers, office supplies, and whatever other support they needed. Some of them did it in one day because it had to be done to survive.

COVID-19 was changing everything. Some of the questions that faced us as a nation and as individuals were as follows: How would our economy recover from the shutdown? How would we on a personal level survive this crisis financially? In April, the government issued $1,200.00 stimulus checks to millions of Americans to provide some financial relief.

Another question was what will happen with our students and the schools? Many schools struggled to have virtual classes. Most schools were just closed. For 2020 graduates at any level, their ring ceremonies, award ceremonies, and graduations were being canceled or postponed.

The pandemic shutdown was affecting everything and everybody—our health, our economy, our education, everything. And the longer we lived in the pandemic, the more of the effects we could see. Working people lost their jobs. We could see the hardship on all but especially the hardship of the poor, the treatment of the poor, and the disparities in health care. We were living through a major crisis. Everything was happening at the same time. We were in need of prayer.

COVID-19 was changing even how people were dying. People were dying every day. Families were forced to do funerals in a totally different way. Rev. Robert Johnson, a United Methodist pastor, shares some of his and his family's experiences with the death of his brother, Tommy Johnson Sr., who died of COVID-19 on March 26, 2020.

On April 1, 2020, Rev. Robert shared on Facebook,

> COVID-19 has changed our way of living. Today we laid my brother to rest. No Funeral Service, no consoling or hugging one another, no viewing of remains, everyone standing around at a distance not to spread the virus. All we could have for my brother was a graveside service for 20 minutes to celebrate his life. Please everyone, take every precaution to protect yourselves.

***

Rev. Robert Johnson and I are pastoral soul mates. The man has a big heart for outreach community ministry. He preaches Jesus Christ to the heart of people. He keeps it "real 100 percent." He can relate to people from all different backgrounds. He is supported in ministry by his wife, Tammy Johnson. During the pandemic, he offered worship services online as well as a Jump Start Prayer from his home that fed me and others. He is the pastor at the Louisiana Ave ("The Ave"), Indian Bayou, and Kaplan United Methodist Churches.

Poem
Category: Healing

The Listener
by
Beatrice Vasser

I went to his grave to talk.
I needed to talk,
someone to listen
without interference.

39

Silence from the dead, visions
portrayed from my heart—
and mind, cautiously imbedded
in shared memories

of love, anxiety, worry and pain,
as I spoke to a person of trust, in
search for wisdom, without a sound of
retained values—entombed in the vault,

as I knelt on my knees in prayer—
with a bouquet of holiday roses
and weeping eyes,
in remembrance of our togetherness.

As I listen for the sound of mercy
A warm touch—gentle with love
A memory etched forever, spiritually
consumed, in the purity of my heart.

***

Beatrice Vasser and I are members of the 126-year-old African American Women Aurora Reading Club of Pittsburgh, Pennsylvania. We enjoy a love for reading. Beatrice W. Vasser received her bachelor of science degree from North Carolina Central and master's and PhD from the University of Pittsburgh. She is the author of *The Circle of Life: Verses from My Journey* (2008) and *The Color of Black* (2015). She has published in *Heart: Dionne's Story,* Volume II (Pittsburgh City Paper, Victorian Ministries; Pink Rose Press) and *Voice from the Attic.*

***

We prayed for each other. We covered the world in prayer. James 5:16 (NRSV) reads, "Therefore confess your sins to one another, and pray for one another. The prayer of the righteous is powerful and effective."

Reflections: Chapter 3

In March 2020, it seemed that the world came to a grinding halt. We were struggling as a country. Were you struggling to find masks, gloves, and hand sanitizer?

1. What else were you struggling with?

2. Most of the country was ordered to stay at home. Did you stay at home? How did it feel to be ordered to stay at home? How did it feel to be at home? What did you do while quarantined at home? If you were/are a front line worker, thank you for your service.

3. Did you pray? Did you seek God? Were you able to worship together in any capacity—phone, social media, computer technology, other?

4. Where did you meet God in the beginning of the 2020 pandemic?

Today's Date:

Where are you convening with God today?

CHAPTER 4

COVID-19 Pandemic Continues

The days on the calendar continued to pass on. I, like many others, joined prayer call-in lines, looking for connection and for inspiration in a variety of places, including Facebook, Twitter, Instagram, and any other social media possible.

The COVID-19 pandemic, staying at home day after day, changed our lives in so many ways. One way was people could not gather together for worship in the physical places and spaces of worship. It changed how we worshipped God and how we did church. Decisions had to be made about Communion, visiting the sick, tithes and offerings, and much more. As now a scattered church, would we worship in our homes? Do we use a call-in number for worship? Do we use Zoom? Do we use Facebook? It was a mad dash of how to keep people together while still being apart. Some pastors and worship leaders had already had virtual worship opportunities available to their congregations; thus a virtual transition was less difficult than for those churches that never did virtual, social media, Zoom, and so on. Use of electronic media for worship? What about Bible study? What about reaching out and caring for the sick and shut-in?

Now most of the church and community was shut-in. Church leaders struggled to find new, different, creative ways to get and keep the scattered church together. Would all of this work, and would it be effective in reaching people in their homes?

Prayer

A Prayer for Pastors
by
Rev. Elenora Mackey Cushenberry, ThD

A prayer in times of disaster or pandemics for shepherds who cannot get to their assigned sheep.

O God,
Heavy is my heart.
I hear the bleating of the sheep
You gave to me.
I hear Jesus' Words

For they are like sheep without a shepherd.
But I am here, O God.
Lead me
Guide me
Show me a way
To reach, without touching
To see, without seeing
To be present, while being distant.
In this I take comfort, O God
And now I am encouraged
That there is nothing that can separate
My shepherd's love for the sheep You have given me
That neither hospitals or nursing homes restrictions
Floods of water or of pandemics
Fires, tornadoes or any force of nature
Will separate my shepherd's love from my assigned flock
That through Your Grace and Mercy
In the Name of Christ Jesus
By the Power of Holy Spirit
I am encouraged.
That my reaching out via call, social media will be felt
That the words You give to me will strengthen the weary soul
Hallelujah! Amen!

Rev. Robert Johnson shared,

Mar 29, 2020 · 🌐

A member sent this to Tammy and me, showing how our Facebook live worship is reaching the children and families in their homes. When I called for altar call this morning during worship, this young girl got on her knees to pray. What an amazing God we serve. We can have church anywhere.

Young Dailee Johnson praying on knees while watching worship on Zoom, March 2020

***

Ten-year-old Dailee Johnson is a member of the Louisiana Avenue United Methodist Church in Lafayette, Louisiana. She and her family visits Mallalieu United Methodist Church in St. Martinville, Louisiana, to worship with her grandparents. She attends St. Martinville Primary School. She loves reading, talking with her grandparents, and gymnastics.

The United Methodist Church ran a campaign called, "Church can happen anywhere!" Its purpose was to remind people that every moment is an opportunity to praise God. The pandemic challenged that concept. Could church and worshipping God really happen anywhere? Could worshipping God happen in our houses? Yes! Church can happen anywhere.

It was April. It was Easter Sunday Morning, and we were having Communion. We had to individually prepare our own Communion. When my church, Mallalieu United Methodist Church, decided we would worship on a call-in line, I decided I would always get up out of bed and get dressed for worship just like I did to go to the physical church building. But today was Easter. Was I going to just get dressed, or was I going to do what I do for Easter? I did what I would normally do for Easter. I wore my Easter hat and outfit at home for worship.

Wearing my Easter hat and outfit as I normally do but now at home in worship, Easter April 2020

I enjoy getting all dressed up and giving God my best for worship especially on the high holy days. I love wearing one of my over one hundred hats. If I thought it was good enough and part of my honoring and worshipping God when I went to the physical church house, then it was good enough and part of my honoring and worshipping God wherever I was at, including inside my house. Worship can happen anywhere. Wearing my Easter hat and outfit helped ground me in how I worshipped God. In many ways, I was angry. Life had changed, but it did not stop. We were living through this challenging time in 2020. The pandemic was changing a lot of things, but I would not allow it to change how my spirit worshipped God with singing and praising and hat wearing and praying. I would not allow a virus to take away those parts of how I worshipped God. My spirit prays to God as I worship. My hat wearing is an outward manifestation of being connected to God, being protected and covered by God. I needed to connect to God the way I connect to God even in the midst of these changes. I needed to connect to my familiar.

Not being at the church physically reminded me of how I worshipped and experienced God when I was away from the actual church building and my family when I lived away from home. Even in the midst of the not normal, I was going to do what I normally did. I would not allow a virus of any size to take away the joy of Easter. Wearing my white hat and dress helped me praise God and weather and brighten the days of the COVID-19 pandemic storm.

And others did not allow the virus to take away their joy of Easter and praising God. Mrs. Tammie Johnson, wife and pastoral supporter, wore her Easter hat and Rev. Johnson his bow tie—they were coordinated and all dressed up.

Rev. Robert Johnson and wife, Tammie, wearing her Easter hat, Easter 2020

Poem
Category: Hope

My Hope Is in You
by
Rev. Tara Sutton

God of Hope,

Each day allows me to be filled with hope. Sometimes, I am downtrodden or disappointed with life, yet when I turn towards you and your word, I gain a sense of hopefulness. Let me find ways to give you the praise even in the small things in life. Help me to be reminded of the joy you give to your children, for the joy of the Lord is our strength. Keep me filled with your hope.

In Christ's Name. Amen

***

Across the world, people were figuring out what would help them with this pandemic: how to live and breathe in this pandemic. Some people cooked. Some people ate more regularly with the people they were quarantined with. My isolated family ate together almost every weekend. We played Phase 10. We had barbecues and crawfish boils. We ate everything in sight. I recognize that many people did not have the support that I am describing here. It was sad that we could not invite others, but we did not want to spread the virus. Family, praying, worshipping God, and wearing my hats were helping me live through the days and the months.

Worshipping and honoring God in the midst of this crisis was what I believed we needed to do. Praying to God in this time is what I believed we needed to do. I was praying, and I wondered if other people were praying. I joined several other prayer lines. I had been praying for the pastors and leaders in the Louisiana Annual Conference of the United Methodist Church. I prayed for Bishop Cynthia Harvey and the district superintendents, Rev. Jan Curwick, Rev. Karli Piegon, Rev. Tom Dolph, and Rev. Wybra Price. I prayed for all the pastors and churches in the Louisiana Conference. I prayerfully decided to write a book of prayers we were praying as we were living through this COVID-19 pandemic. I wasted no time.

In April, Easter had come and gone, and we were still isolated in our homes. I wrote a letter inviting friends, family, and colleagues to send me prayers, poems, and pictures of them and family wearing hats, which I would include in the book. In the letter, I indicated that the proceeds from the sale of this book would go to the Orphe Generational Foundation (OGF).

Also in April, my sorority chapter president, Mary Carter, asked me to lead our chapter in prayer every Wednesday at 12:15 p.m. All the prayers that I wrote that appear in this book were prayed with the women from my sorority chapter. I began to pray and received prayers for a cure of the virus, comfort for families who lost loved ones to this virus, and recovery and healing for those fighting the virus. Our focus was on praying for the end of this COVID-19 virus. We covered each other in prayer.

Prayer
First Wednesday Prayer Call, April 15, 2020

Easter Has Come and Gone, but Stay at Home
John 20:20
by
Rev. Martha Orphe

Easter has come and gone but Lord you are still making your Resurrection Presence known throughout the world.

In the Gospel of **John 20:20**, that first Easter, the disciples were in the house, they were at home. You went to them, you went to the house. You were with them. As we continue to stay home, isolated, separated physically from others, let us remember that we are not alone, you are with us. **Jesus you are with us at our house, in our homes**. Let us feel your presence. The scriptures say that they were filled with joy when you were with them. Lord, in the midst of everything we are experiencing, let us feel your joy. **Let us praise you anyhow, anyway, anywhere!** That in the darkness of these times, we can still rejoice, we can still be your light, we can even still be happy!! We know that it's going to get better in Jesus' Holy and Matchless Name! Hallelujah! Hallelujah! Hallelujah! Amen.

Reflections: Chapter 4

Staying at home continued. Washing hands and social distancing became a part of our lives. The pandemic was changing a lot of things.

1. What did it change in your life in 2020?

2. Did you try to connect with God, your family, and your friends?

3. Did you join others in prayer? How?

4. What was your hat, your familiar, your comfort? What helped you get through the early part of the 2020 health pandemic?

Today's Date:

How has prayer impacted your life today?

Read John 20:20. Are there any similarities in the events in the Bible and the events that happened in 2020?

CHAPTER 5

COVID-19 Continued On and On

Reflection
by
Rev. Clifton Conrad Sr.

Good morning beloved!

As we enter into a time of prayer, let us take time to consider the power of (both dunamis and exousia) that has been granted by God's throne, the Holy Spirit. Through prayer, geographical boundaries are shattered, as we pray for others around the world. Through prayer, healings are accomplished. Through prayer, people are comforted in what seems to be hopeless situations. Let us not forget 2 Chronicles 7:14 and the power of collective prayer. How has prayer impacted your life today?

Gracious and loving God, as we humble ourselves before you, this morning, we thank you for this opportunity to be in prayer. Bless those who we name in our hearts this morning. Guide us by the power of your mighty hand, as we go through this day. In the name of Jesus we pray. Amen.

Prayer

A Breath Prayer
by
Rev. Elenora Mackey Cushenberry, ThD

I am (You are),
Covered in the Blood
of Jesus for protection from within and without.
Covered in the Peace of Jesus
for peace in the midst of internal and external strife.
Covered with the mind of Jesus

for an answer for Self and for Others.
Covered with the knowledge of Jesus
to remind me
I am never Alone
I am more than a conqueror (I am a victor)
I am equipped for this Day
In the Name of Christ Jesus, by the Power of the Holy Spirit. Amen.

Prayer

A Call for Prayer–COVID 19
by
Rev. Darlene Moore

Most Loving God, today, I_____ am saying a bold prayer, studying a believable Holy Word of God—The Bible, and standing blissfully on God's promises. Black Lives are dying, doomed, depressed, disobedient, and we need you now, God!! We Pray, O God, the expectancy of your power helps the forgotten, fought, and fearful, soon. In Jesus Name, Amen.

Rev. Darlene Moore, parents, Mrs. Dolores and Mr. Charles Moore, and grandsons, Jeremiah and Joshua, III

Rev. Darlene "Showers of Blessings" Moore is a prayer warrior pastor who calls and prays with me. She is the pastor at St. Peter-Trinity and Asbury United Methodist Churches in Jeanerette, Louisiana. Her mother, Mrs. Dolores Ada Moore, may she rest in peace, was well cared for by her daughter. Rev. Moore was her father's caregiver until Mr. Charles Clinton Moore passed away February 10, 2021. Rev. Moore enjoys the company of grandsons Jeremiah Joshua James, seven years old, and Joshua III, six years old, who love riding their bikes, fishing, roller skating, dogs, and dinosaurs. Their parents are Yolanda James and the late Joshua James II.

Prayer

Front Line Worker Prayer
by
Rev. Darlene Moore

Most Loving God, I, _____ am petitioning You, O Wise God, to help all frontline workers, truckers, and clergy, school teachers, and their families. God, I, _____ am asking you, to keep them and their families safe, healthy, encouraged, and COVID 19 free. God, I, _____ also need you to protect their families, friends, finances, and faith. Also, I, _____, pray God, You, keep the frontline workers healthy, wealthy, expectant, and encouraged. Please, God, help our hospitals and hurting schools and sanctuaries to be HEALED!

Prayer

Three Things We Should Do to Navigate Successfully COVID-19
by
Rev. Darlene Moore

Pray Up
Mask Up
Speak UP
God help us to daily do things three, believing and claiming HEALING. Amen.

Reflection

God Has Smiled on Me
by
Rev. Clifton Conrad Sr.

Good morning beloved!

As we face the start of a new day, let us look to the east and see God's smile in the rising of the sun. There is a song that says, "God has smiled on me—He has set me free. God has smiled on me—He's been good to me." Enjoy the goodness of the Lord this day.

May all that occurs in your life today be turned over to God. Let us thank God for God's goodness and God's mercy. Let us thank God for being with us to see us through every problem we may face. Let us praise God for making it possible for us to have life beyond this life. *In the name of Jesus we pray. Amen and Amen.*

***

Day after day and now month after month, the isolation and separation were settling in on us in the month of May, and they were wearing most of us thin with the anxiety, the stress, the unknown, and the uncertainties.

In the month of May for Mother's Day, we were still at home for worship. I did what I would normally do for Mother's Day. I wore a Mother's Day hat and outfit at my home for worship. How would we honor our mothers or be honored as mothers in this new way of living?

May 2020, Mother's Day hat and outfit
Bright and joyous purple

Jan Dupuy's mother, Mrs. Williemeaner Anderson

Prayer

A Prayer for Mothers
by
Janice A. Dupuy

Dear Lord, you know a mother's heart is a battlefield of wars won, lost, but never surrendered. **We come to you each and every day asking favor not for ourselves but for our children.** We pray for our unborn children. We pray for our children born into this world. Most gracious God, we pray you **sustain those of us who must endure the infinite grief and pain of losing a child.** Help mothers trust in your wisdom. Give them strength and courage to face each day. All-knowing God, hear the prayers of mothers and heal their broken hearts.

Jan Dupuy
"Live a grateful life!"
Alpha Gamma Zeta Chapter New Orleans
Zeta Phi Beta Sorority, Inc.
No Greater Love Sister Circles 1 and 2

No Greater Love is the name of the sister circle because there is no greater love than a mother who has lost a son. Member of the sister circle sorority sister Dawn Collins lost her military son Caleb, and both her biological and sorority sister Rita Arceneaux lost her son to a car accident.

Prayer

A Mother's Prayer
by
Dolores Edwards

O Heavenly Father I come to you, humble, as a mother to pray for our children.

O Heavenly Father, I pray for their past, present and future.

O Heavenly Father, protect them from seen and unseen danger.

O Heavenly Father, thank you for everything; thank you for waking them up to a brand new day.

O Heavenly Father, **protect our children** from peer pressure and let them be around positive people.

O Heavenly Father, thank you for all your love and care.

O Heavenly Father, thank you for your daily covering.

O Heavenly Father, I know you will protect our children as they walk through their **daily lives.**

O Heavenly Father, lay your hands on them to protect and guide them

O Heavenly Father, don't let our children lose sight of your words

O Heavenly Father a mother's love knows that the will of God will never take our children where the Grace of God will not protect them.

A Prayer of a Mother's Love
Dedicated to my number one fan, my mother, Soror Lola Tilton
From Soror Dolores Edwards

Dolores Tilton-Edwards and her mother, Lola Tilton

***

Dolores Tilton-Edwards and her mom, Lola Tilton, are some of the sweetest quiet spirits that I know. We are sisters in Christ and sorority sisters. Dolores is a retired United States postal worker. She enjoys looking at TV and tutoring her grandchildren in math.

Lola Tilton is a retired math teacher. She enjoys traveling all over the world.

Mallalieu Church members Becky Cole and daughter, Megan

Becky and I are members of the Mallalieu United Methodist Church. Megan was reared in the church. Megan now has a family of her own, and she and her husband are raising their children in Mallalieu Church. The young family stayed connected to the church and to God through the 2020 pandemic.

Top photo: Mrs. Erma Tyler, Wonda Crawford
Lower photo: Tracey Powell and her mother, Mrs. Ardist Moses

Some of my sorority sisters: Erma Tyler, Wonda Crawford, and Tracey Powell
Mrs. Ardist Moses
July 30, 1934–January 4, 2021

People were honoring their mothers in 2020 in very different ways. Visitation of elderly mothers, or anyone else, in nursing homes was not permitted. COVID ran rampant in many nursing homes, and numerous of the residents died. Some families never had the opportunity to say goodbye to their dying nursing home family member.

Poem
Presented July 2020 at hat fundraiser

Haiku: Missing Motherdear
by
Dr. Rosalind Hale

Missing Motherdear
She smiles when I sleep.
We talk when I am awake.
Now I cry inside.

Forgotten never.
Loved always and forever.
Meaningful lessons.

Purposeful memories
Meant to make me smile and cry.
Although I still grieve.
Grieving and healing,
must partner together now
for meaningful life.

Lessons and life lived.
She taught me how to be strong.
Motherdear is missed.

***

Dr. Hale is my wonderful mentor, sorority sister, and prayer partner. She is a talented poet. She invited me to join the Monday evening 8:46 Prayer Campaign prayer line to pray for our land.

Dr. Rosalind Pijeaux Hale, Xavier University of Louisiana, is a retired professor emeritus, Division of Education and Counseling, Educational Leadership; Zeta Phi Beta Sorority, Inc., Alpha Rho Zeta

Chapter, Tamias Grammateus, Diamond life member; Dove; past SC regional director; past national trustee; past Zeta National Educational Foundation, Inc.; board member; and current International Women of Color Committee member.

Day after day in the month of May, we continued to pray, and the prayers continued to come to my email, except now the prayers were not just about a cure for the COVID-19 virus and those dying and in recovery.

Prayer

Standing in Need
by
Rev. Deborah Williams

How excellent is your name in all the earth. We come today in humility and thanksgiving. We come knowing that we are not worthy to be in your presence. But still we come with hearts full of thanksgiving because you are the only help we know. All we have ever needed, you have provided.

Lord, we are standing in the need of your healing. Touch us with your healing power and make us whole. We are standing in the need of your justice. Your children are being shot to death in their homes, smothered in the street and shot in the back for no reason than the color of their skin. May your justice roll down like a river and righteousness like a mighty stream!

We are standing in the need of your peace and comfort. Give us your peace that passes all understanding. May we feel your comforting presence! We are standing in the need of your protection. Please watch our going out and coming in.

Most all Lord we are standing in the need of forgiveness. Forgive us Lord when we have failed to love as you called us to love and to serve as you have called us to serve. Free us for joyful obedience to your will and your way. Empower us to be steadfast and immovable in our faith. We pray all these things in the matchless name of your Son, Jesus. Amen.

***

Rev. Deborah is a justice-praying, fighting pastor friend of mine. We have fought many battles together as clergywomen. Rev. Williams, MDiv, is the pastor of Hartzell Mt. Zion United Methodist Church in Slidell, Louisiana.

Reflections: Chapter 5

The COVID virus is like the uninvited guest who refuses to leave. People continued to get sick and people continued to die.

1. Do you know someone who contracted the virus? Did you lose family or friends to the virus? Did you seek sustenance from God?

2. The pandemic caused businesses to shut their doors or reduce capacity. Many people became bored and impatient. Some wanted to reenter society and restart the economy. How did you feel? What did you do?

3. Were you a graduating student or did you know graduating students? How did you respond to the 2020 nontraditional graduating year? Did your community establish workarounds for canceled occasions, such as proms, award ceremonies, and graduation ceremonies?

4. Everyone one was impacted by COVID. It was especially difficult for nursing home facilities and residents. People were dying, and family members did not have an opportunity to say goodbye. Did you know anyone who lived or worked in a nursing home? If you are a nursing home worker, thank you for your service.

CHAPTER 6

George Floyd

On May 25, the world watched in horror as George Floyd pleaded, "I can't breathe!" and cried out for his mother. If we, the people around the world and the people in the United States, did not have enough trouble living through the uncertainties of the COVID-19 virus, now the killing of this Black man, George Floyd, by white police officer Derek Chauvin, brought about yet more calls for justice and to stop the killing of innocent Black and Brown people by the police—stop the police brutality and recognize that Black Lives Matter.

And so we covered each other in prayer.

Prayer
Wednesday Prayer Call, May, 27, 2020

"I Can't Breathe"
by
Rev. Martha Orphe

Lord, God, **we are hurting real bad right now**. We are angry; and mad. We pray for the direction of this country and our lives. We want to be treated fairly and equally. We want to live in peace. We want to breathe.

Lord God, let me testify. I live on 24/7 oxygen and I am grateful to be alive. Lord, I know when I can't breathe. George Floyd said, "I can't breathe!" We know when we can't breathe. We know you are the air we breathe in and out. Hear us as we pray and hear us as we breathe your air in and out, in and out!! Almighty, No One, No other person has the right to stop your free God given air that we breathe. God, no human being has the right until I say so, to take me off the Portable Oxygen Concentrator (POC) Air that provides me the Air I breathe. No other human being has the right to take away the air we breathe in and out, in and out. **No other person has the right to put their knee on our neck and take away our God given air away from us.** We want to breathe. We want to live. We want to live in peace. We want to love. We want to know your love and hope and your comfort today. For you are our Comforter.

Lord, we are praying today for change to come. **We pray for President Trump.** Lord help him to see what is needed for all the people in the country and not just for some of the people. Lord, we are praying for a change. We pray for the safety of the Protestors and the Marches. **We pray for the Police Officers who do not seek to harm, hurt or kill us but rather seek to protect us. Protect them and their families. Lord, we pray for a change of heart and mind of those Police Officers who want to harm, hurt, and even kill us because of the color of our skin.** Almighty God we know that only you can bring about the Peace, Justice, Love and Community. Help us to strive harder and harder for your Beloved Community on this Earth in this place. Help us Lord to do our part every day.

Lord, let us remember the air we breathe in and out with every breath we take. Let us use it to better the world. When the air, the oxygen oxygenates any part of our bodies, let us use it for the good of all humankind. Use our hands to push a button to vote. Use our knees to pray. Use our minds to generate questions, make plans and policies. Use our mouths to voice our concerns and demands. Use our bodies to be a human shield, if necessary, for our families, friends, and/or another human being in need of protection. Let us use our lives to Glorify You, O God, we pray. **We just want to breathe and live for you.**

Amen and Amen.

***

Upon the invitation of Mary Carter, I joined the St. Joseph Missionary Baptist Church's early morning prayer line. I was leading prayers, but I knew my spirit needed to hear more from God through other pastors. Rev. Melvin C. Zeno was one of the pastors who fed my aching, lamenting soul with their prayers.

Prayer

8 Minutes, 46 seconds
by
Rev. Dr. Cynthia Belt

Spirit Wind is blowing, but **we can't breathe**.
Spirit words are flowing but speech is beyond us, we can't breathe.
Collectively we hold our breath, **we strain against the need for oxygen**, and then we gasp.
We, people of faith, gasp in the hope of Spirit breath and Spirit words
and with each gasp, we re-commit ourselves to life:

**And so we honor our ancestor George Floyd and all the ancestors
sacrificed on the altar of white supremacy with:**
8 minutes, 46 seconds of kindness each day
8 minutes, 46 seconds to commit to acts of justice
8 minutes, 46 seconds to breathe deeply, each breathe a reminder of the life of our communities
8 minutes, 46 seconds to call the names of all those who are victims of state sanctioned violence
8 minutes, 46 seconds to say a prayer, even so come Lord Jesus.
And so it is. Ase'

***

Rev. Dr. Cynthia Belt and I have known each other for over thirty years. We have worked together to support clergywomen in the United Methodist Church at all levels, including praying and working for the election of women as bishops. We know the power of covering church leaders in prayer. We have prayed and worked together for justice throughout the United States and across the world because we believe in the power of prayer and the power of putting our faith into action.

Rev. Cynthia Belt, M.Div, D.Min, pastors Mt. Zion and Harwood United Methodist Churches in Laurel and Elkridge, Maryland, respectively. Dr. Belt is a contributing author in the book *Sister to Sister*, Volume 2, edited by Dr. Linda Hollies. She is a contributing author to the books *God's Promises for Women of Color* and *The Women of Color Study Bible*. She serves on the board of directors for *Precious Times* magazine and has written several articles for that publication. Most recently, she contributed an essay to the book *The Black Church and Hip Hop Culture*, edited by Dr. Emmett T. Price of Northeastern University. She enjoys hanging out with her granddaughter, jewelry making, and writing. She is in several organizations: Order of Elders, United Black Clergy of Anne Arundel County, Black Clergywomen of the United Methodist Church, and Black Methodist Church Renewal.

Prayer
Wednesday Prayer Call, June 3, 2020

Holy Mary, Mother of God
by
Rev. Orphe

Holy Mary, Mother of God, pray for us now in this hour

Holy Mary, Mother of God, pray for us in this hour.

You prayed for your son as he was hanging on the cross, brutalized, stretched wide, head hung down, blood pouring, gushing down his side. **You prayed for your son as he died right before your eyes.**

Lord, God almighty, Heavenly Father, Good, good father, you looked down and saw your son dying on that cross right before your eyes.

Holy Mary, Mother of God, Heavenly Father, hear us as we pray for our sons and daughters being killed, murdered right before our eyes. Hear us as we pray, hear us as we mourn. Heavenly Father, it is written in the Bible that if we pray, you will hear our prayers. Psalm 116:1. Your son David cried out to you, "I love the Lord, he heard my cry," each and every one. Lord Jesus, we love you and pray you are hearing all our prayers.

Lord, as if it was not enough that the COVID-19 virus is killing more of us African Americans than any other group of people in this country, we are still losing our sons and daughters to hate crimes, police brutality, cold blooded murders. Lord, we continue to pray for a stop of this deadly virus, but Lord we have been praying for a long time for the killings to stop.

Lord, as people of color make a larger percentage of essential workers in this country, trying to make a living, trying to protect others, and yet, even their lives are on the frontline daily to be the next African American, Person of Color, to be killed by such senseless killings by the hands of those who are called to serve and protect us.

Lord God Almighty hear our anger, hear our desperation, hear our bleeding hearts as we ask you, how long this will continue on? Our ancestors prayed these prayers. Our parents prayed these prayers. We are praying these prayers. Our children are praying these prayers. Will our children's children pray these prayers? Will our children's, children's, children pray these prayers? Make it stop Lord, make them stop. Stop the senseless killings, Stop the evil, and the taking of innocent life.

Help us to help others see that our lives matter, that you O God did not make a mistake when you chose to create us in your beautiful Black, Noir skin color.

Lord, may the sunflower in the garden be as beautiful as the lily in the garden. You created and made them all and made all of us, Black, White, Red, Yellow, Brown, you made us all your children and we all are precious in your sight.

Lord, we have talked among ourselves. We have protested and marched. We have called for legal action, legislative actions, and we have called for justice. Let justice roll down like only you can make it happen.

Lord God we are feeling it today. We are fragile like clay jars, earthen vessels. Remind us that the Power, the love, the peace comes from you and not from us. Lord, if we keep it real and tell you the truth, of what you already see in our hearts, some of us may want to kill, retaliate, hurt and/or harm somebody. But remind us as it is found in 2 Corinthians 4:8–9, "we are hard pressed on every side, but not crushed, perplexed, but not in despair, persecuted, but not abandoned, struck down, but not destroyed."

Holy Mary, Mother of God, pray for us in this hour!

Lord Jesus, hear us as we pray. Amen.

Reflection

Reflection
by
Rev. Clifton Conrad Sr.

Good morning beloved!

The historic nature of the times in which we find ourselves make me wonder how this will be written in the annals of time. Will it be seen as the time when people turned toward God, or away from God wondering how God could allow a biological virus to infect our physical health and the spiritual virus of racism and injustice to affect our social order? My faith moves me to trust God. How about you?

Gracious God, You hold all things in Your almighty and powerful hands. You order this thing we call life. Lord, as we enter this day, may our faith and Your grace and mercy be with us as we face whatever may come our way. We will praise You in the Good and trust you in the bad situations of our journey. We thank You for all that we will go through, because we know You are with us. In the name of Jesus we pray. Amen.

Prayer

Unfinished Pentecost Prayer of Sorts
by
Rev. Paulette Brown
Toronto, Canada

Breathe: Today we receive the Breath of God, the Spirit rages, disturbs, converts and consoles.

Breath of God: What does it mean to claim this?

Surely it means ending the white supremacy that murderously takes breath away.

Surely it means guarding, with dignity, the breath of our elders until its natural end.

Surely it means giving every virus ravaged body equal access to the care that will sustain breath.

Surely it means celebrating every baby's first breath—whether in Juba, Grassy Narrows or Manila—with equity and possibility.

Breath of the Divine, what does it mean to claim this? What does it mean … And what will I do? What

***

Rev. Paulette Brown lives in Toronto, Canada. Twenty years ago, I met her at a black clergywomen conference in Atlanta. She and others saw the invitation to this conference and flew to the United States not knowing anyone. Since that moment, Rev. Paulette has been friend and family. Her family is my family, and my family is her family—especially in the difficult year of 2020. She is the voice for justice. She is the pastor at St. Andrew's Humber Heights Presbyterian Church in Canada.

Jamaican Canadians Rev. Eleanor Scarlett and Rev. Paulette Brown with Rev. Martha.
We have been supporting each other in justice ministries for over 20 years.

Reflection
June 7, 2020
Excerpt of a sermon at Bolton United Church, Ontario, Canada

By Reverend Eleanor Scarlett

Since the middle of March, we have been **huddled down at home** and have not been able to gather face to face **because of COVID19**. Yet we have found ways to stay connected and to be nurtured by means of different forms of technologies. **Like others, I too miss the personal connections**. I miss being in church, seeing your faces, hearing your laughter, and sharing in your stories.

Some of us have found creative ways on how to use this time of social isolation wisely. Since last week, **my sister and I have been gardening.** This offers us some semblance of wellbeing as we reconnect with Mother Earth as a gift of God's creation. Despite trying to find common grounds on **how to live into this time of social isolation, I want you to know that the current issues around racism, racial justice and racial inequalities have been weighing heavily on my heart.**

Some of you might say but it is not here it is in another country, it's not our problem. Yes, it is true, **but I want to remind you that racism and racial injustices are alive and well in Canada also**. I have watched the video over and over again of a Police Officer lynching of George Floyd an African American man; I cannot get it out of my soul. How can another human being sit on the neck of another person and crush him to death with his knees? Is it because he views this individual not as a person, not as a human being, not as a creation of God but rather as something worthy to be killed. Or could it be that Black Lives does not matter!

George Floyd cried I am thirsty, he cried I can't breathe, the cry that broke me, was the cry for his mama. When a grown man cries for his dead mama you know he is in deep trouble. The haunting cries for his mama will live with me forever. I remember that first cry for thirst, it came from a cross where an innocent man's body and soul was being brutalized by the political and religious systems. Yes, Jesus cried, "I am thirsty," George Floyd cried, "I am thirsty." Eric Gardener cried, "I am thirsty." How many more must cry "I am thirsty?" When will it stop? My heart is heavy.

I am hurting, I am angry, I can't sleep, I am sick and tired of seeing these images on TV. I am sick and tired of hearing families crying in agony for their loved ones, killed by Police Officers who are called to serve and protect. Just over a month ago, D'Andre Campbell called Police because he knew that he was having a mental health meltdown. They entered his home, shot, and killed him in front of his family.

How then do we move through these situations? Here I am crying out, am I weak for doing so, am I not a good pastor for reaching out to others, has anyone in authority asked me how I am doing? I am grateful for some wonderful friends and colleagues who have reached out to me, who have checked in, to see how I am doing: I am thankful for your caring. Yet I find these words playing out in my head, the late Dr. Martin Luther King Jr said, "In the end we will remember not the words of our enemies, but the silence of our friends."

This virus has also exposed racial inequalities amongst us. We watch the heart wrenching pains on the faces of families as they grieve the loss of their loved ones across this country. As a country we can no longer turn a blind eye, we must call our political and religious leaders to repent.

***

I met Rev. Eleanor Scarlett at the same conference in Atlanta some twenty years ago when I met Rev. Paulette Brown. We met, and Rev. Eleanor became family. Her family is my family, and my family is her family. She is the voice of justice. She is the pastor at Bolton United Church in Bolton, Ontario. She and the family live in Brampton, Ontario, where she enjoys reading, cooking, gardening, walking, and hanging out with her dogs, Bailey and Diva.

All across America's cities and towns, people were experiencing these real live events and reacting in different ways. But it was not just in the United States. Just as a child in England was experiencing the real live event of COVID-19, people across the world were also experiencing the same real live event of the killing of George Floyd. Rev. Paulette Brown and Rev. Eleanor Scarlett of Canada spoke the prophetic truth to the people in Canada as some pastors preached the truth in the United States. In both countries, questions were asked about the religious and church leaders who were silent.

Prayer

Respect
by
Rev. Farrell Narcisse

Dear heavenly Father, I praise You for all the things You have done for me, but I honor You, for who you are, my Lord and King. May I always show respect for the whole family of God, as I know that is one way I can honor you. Help me to be sensitive and respectful to all people, no matter what position they hold. Lord, deliver Your people from all prejudice and disrespect for one another. May we obey Your Word that tells us to prefer and honor one another, as brothers and sisters in the Lord. May we also be especially kind toward those who are in occupations in the service sector and may we all serve one another. I ask this in the name of Jesus. Amen.

***

Rev. Farrell Narcisse and I went to St. Martinville Senior High school in St. Martinville, Louisiana. I left home and returned some forty years later. I reconnected with Rev. Farrell through his Facebook prayers. As a long-haul truck driver, he posts these prayers from the various cities he travels to across the United States. He has preached at my home church, and we have prayed for people through text messaging. Rev. Farrell is a praying man. His prayers have been part of the morning devotion for me as well as many others.

The COVID-19 pandemic, racially based police killings, and hatred-based violence was on the rise again. People are tired. Black and Brown people and some others are tired of the hate, the negativity, and the chaos. All of the killings bring up our past griefs and sorrow. It's like living in a constant state of grief. We are downright sick and tired and have had enough. Enough is enough. People are tired, frustrated, exhausted.

Some peaceful protests were met with force by the police. Riots were met with force by the police. The prayers continue to ask for justice day after day and now month after month into the summer.

Say Their Names

George Floyd
Breonna Taylor
Ahmaud Arbery
Sandra Bland
Michael Brown
Tony McDade

Say all their names.

What should we do?
Join others in prayer.
Get in "Good Trouble."
Organize and/or Participate in Peaceful Protest.
Let Justice Roll

Prayer

What Do I Do When …
by
Rev. John Winn

The Spirit of the Lord is upon me, because he has anointed me to bring good news to the poor. He has sent me to proclaim release to the captives and recovery of sight to the blind, to let the oppressed go free, to proclaim the year of the Lord's favor. Luke 4:18–19 Jesus' first sermon in his hometown.

O Dear God,

What do I do when the good news seems wrapped in a virus and violence is offered as an answer?
What do I do when many are held captive by leaders who cannot sense the beam in their own eyes,
themselves blinded by power and pretense, ending lives of the oppressed with knees to their necks?

I am driven to my own knees for there seems to be no place else to go. My prayers are joined with others
from my own family, my friends, their friends, people none of us know, choirs of prayer, communities
of prayer, the sound of them growing louder, louder, and louder until my whole being shudders and my
knees are aching with the weight of prayers. **I realize I must get up, I must stand** with the captives,
stand with the blind who cannot see, stand with the oppressed, live with them, know them, love them,
yes, love them, and by your grace love them and all of us back to life.

This is the cycle we know, the truth we know to be self-evident, the truth on which a nation can be born,
and when necessary, reborn. We will need help, O Lord, we will need the best that is within us, in the
name of the One who has shown us the way, the truth, and the life.

Amen

#BLACKLIVESMATTER

Dr. Kim Dauterive, family, and friends
at a peaceful protest
June 2020

Kimberly Poppas Mom Dauterive wrote, "I feel so proud to have been a part of this peaceful protest! There was REAL UNITY from start to finish. Everyone was on ONE ACCORD and STANDING TOGETHER against racism, injustice and prejudice. Seeing this and being a part of it has increased my HOPE! God is always on time!"

***

Dr. Kim Smith Dauterive and I have known each other first as fellow church members and sisters in Christ. We continue now as patient, doctor, Divine 9 Sister (AKA), and friends. Dr. Kimberly Smith Dauterive, MD, is a board certified internist. She is the owner of JKL Healthcare Services located in New Iberia, Louisiana. Her offices are filled with gospel music and scripture, providing a warm Christian atmosphere.

Reflection
by
Rev. Clifton Conrad Sr.

Good morning beloved!

As we greet the morning my prayers go out to ALL of the protesters, both the peaceful and the not so peaceful. No one should lose their life for looting. I pray for the people who wear the badge and are sworn to protect and serve and for those who have violated that oath. I pray for the National Guard, who have been put in the precarious position of enforcing law to serve a political means. Lord, hear our prayers!

Lord, when we feel helpless, You become our strength. When we are oppressed, You deliver us. When the spiritual wickedness shackles us, You set us free. As we journey through this day, we look to You and trust You as our healer, comforter and redeemer. In the name of Jesus we pray. Amen.

Prayer

Let Justice Roll
by
Rev. Paulette Brown

Preaching Amos 5:18–24.

No hiding place from God's anger when we are silent on injustice. Amos says we run from the lion—get cornered by the bear—run from bear into safety of home—get bitten by snake. No hiding place! One option. Let justice flow not like the trickle of a faulty tap. Nor water that forms a puddle and breeds mosquitoes. **Let justice flow like NIAGARA FALLS** as my African Canadian colleague the Rev. Ralston Mitchell would say.

Prayer
Category: Social Unrest

Black Mandemic
by
Beatrice Vasser

Black Mandemic
Term originated by Beatrice Vasser
Wear A Mask—
This virus is the color of the skin.
The Black face is the mask, not protection,
but elicit death by lynching, beating, shooting,
prevalent in every state in the union.

Social distancing—
Segregation rules and regulations—forced to the ghetto,
reservations, schools, work, homes, & recreation facilities.
Avoidances in buying homes, positions and economical gains.
one percent black blood laws written, linger today.

Wash your hands—
They are not clean—cannot wash the demon away.
The Black Mandemic is a contagious infection—
in the heart and brain of the white power demeanor—
searching for wealth and control to succeed.

Poem

My Words
by
Rev. Dr. Cynthia Belt

For idle words and Careless words
For biting words and cutting words
Forgive me

For mean spirited words, and nasty words
For hateful words, and spiteful words
Forgive me

For jealous words and envious words
For resentful words and bitter words
Forgive me

For gossiping words and slandering words
For malicious words and mocking words
Forgive me

For words unspoken and words unheard,
Words withheld and lying words
Forgive me

Temper my heart and temper my tongue
For loving words and compassionate words
For encouraging words and uplifting words
For forgiving words and giving words

This is my prayer

Prayer
Category: Hope

Vengeance Is Mine
by
Dr. Kimberly Smith Dautrieve, MD

"All things work together for the good of those who love the Lord."
Romans 8:28 (NKJV)

Father God please let me be constantly reminded of your power and might especially when it seems like evil is prevailing. Increase my Faith! Show up and show out! Help me to always remember that no matter how grim or unfair a situation appears to be, You will always have the last word and You will never forsake your children! I trust you Lord!

Prayer

Wisdom
by
Rev. Farrell Narcisse

Dear heavenly Father, I do appreciate the sound advice and wisdom found in the book of Proverbs. Lord, help me to apply this advice to situations in my daily life when I am faced with certain issues. Lord Jesus, give me Your discernment to know how I should relate to certain people who irritate me or bother me in some way. May I respond to them in love and in wisdom. May I know the difference when I am approached by someone with an honest heart or someone who is manipulating me for the wrong purposes. Fill my mouth with wisdom in these cases. I ask this in the name of the Lord Jesus. Amen.

Prayer

A Prayer from My Heart in 2020
by
Rev. Dr. Ouida Lee

... Oh God, it seems that we are living through very difficult times. Yet, O God, I am comforted that you have promised that you will never leave, nor forsake us. As we look out on the landscape of our society, we are facing the twin pandemic of Covid19 and Racism. We come before you today and invite you to walk with us. Death seems to be coming to us on every hand and so many are dying in the hospitals alone without the comfort of our families. We are so thankful that you are a Holy God and move by the power of your Holy Spirit. Thank you for being with our loved ones who find themselves dying alone. We stand on your promise that even though we do not see you, you are there.

Comfort our broken hearts as we grieve the loss of ones so dear to us. And Lord, we do not understand death, but we take this journey believing in your truth that earth has no sorrow that heaven cannot heal. Oh God comfort those who are mourning today, give them the assurance that you are our ever-present help in our every hour of need.

We pray for our health care workers, nurses and doctors and those who are on the frontlines taking care of all who are in the hospitals and the Care Facilities. Protect them from the viruses and give them the vision and the patience to walk through this time. Make their hands healing hands and provide for them all of the strength that they need to endure. And the vaccine that is coming, allow it to offer healing and protection for all.

We pray for the people who are suffering the pandemic of Racism. We have seen it raise its head in the midst of issues that affect our lives. It is alive in the hearts of those who believe that it is their right and privilege to be favored because of the color of their skin. We ask for your divine intervention on behalf of our young Black men who are simply trying to make their way through life. We pray protection over each and every one of them who are simply going about life and are attacked because of the prejudice that exists within the hearts of those who are sworn to protect us. Dear God we ask for your divine intervention. Teach us O God not to simply talk about love, but to live the Agape Love of Jesus Christ.

Dear God, we pray for every church door that stands open in your name. We lift every Pastor and member before you so that we do not lose faith during the time that we are sequestered at home. May we take this time to spend with our families, our children and bring us all closer to you?

Bless our children who are attempting to be homeschooled by parents and grandparents who are doing their best. You truly are the way, the truth and the light. We ask special provisions for those who have lost so much during this time, employment, homes, forcing them to beg for food and sustenance. God only You. Our hearts are broken as we listen to the news and see the desperate faces of those who are doing their best to hang on. Give vision to new leaders and supportive, cooperative spirits. And break the domination and control and show us how to walk together. Teach us how to lay aside the sin and the very weights that separate us. You are our God and we trust you with all of our hearts and we do not lean on our own understanding, but we come knowing that you are well able to direct our paths.

Oh God, we pray for unity in our nation. We pray for the leaders of our country, empower them with your peace, power and anointing with a spirit of cooperation so that we may heal our nation. You have taught us O God that, "If your people who are called by your name would humble themselves and pray, turn from their wicked ways, then I will hear from heaven and forgive their sin and heal their land." God we are calling for a humbling and a healing.

We need you God to walk into our Political arena, into the justice system, into the hospitals, into the prisons and protect and direct your people. Most of all, we need you to open the hearts and the minds of understanding to walk with You, O God. Create within our nation today dear God the spirit of surrender to your will and your way. And we will always, always give all praise, glory and honor to you, in the name of Jesus. Amen.

Shown in picture: Dr. Ouida Lee, Mrs. Shahida Tross Nuriddin, Rev. Martha, Mrs. Nina Nuriddin-Hodges, and Iman Wayne Ali Nurridin, some of our interfaith friends

***

Dr. Lee is my dear clergy sister friend. We have prayed, cried, and rejoiced together. We have traveled together and prayed for the world together. Rev. Dr. Ouida F. Lee is a retired elder in the North Texas Annual Conference of the United Methodist Church.

Mrs. Shahida ("Sha") Nurridin is my Muslim mother and friend. Nina Nurridin-Hodges is my sister and my friend. Imam Wayne Ali Nurridin is my colleague, brother, and friend. The Nurridin Family, Mr. Thomas Ali Nurridin (deceased), Mrs. Shahida, Nina, and Imam Wayne Ali Nurridin, work tirelessly with their Masjid Bilal Community in New Orleans. They also worked with me and my churches for years as we did interfaith ministries together in the city of New Orleans, including prayer services and community outreach. They covered me with their prayers, and I covered them with my prayers.

Poem
Category: Hope

Flying out of Slavery–High above the Spirit Tree
by
Beatrice Vasser

After *The Invention of Wings* by Sue Monk Kidd
(Mauma gives hope to Hetty to fly out of slavery)

My heart beats fast of fear and shame.
it beats fast because I am woman. It
berates, dishonors the humane in me—
worst than an animal of equal homage.

Tired in bondage, with no dissent
subservient to use—for work or pleasure
use of a body without a mind (or consent)
beguile—gives power and control to others.

Punished, beaten, hung regardless of age
welps, branding, one-legges choke-as straps
lossen the swollen legs, bulging eyes, bleeding,
a head images of freedom—a flight of freedom.

My spirit lives high—in limbs of the old oak tree
watching, planning, and scheming—denotes an
humiliate soul—full of the pains of hurt and hate,
penniless broken—for the sake of economic gains.

Secrets hidden in defiant and deceit, subversive
Thoughts without a voice—buried in the belly of
The Story Quilt—wearing a pouch without wings,
Which wards off the saga of slavery twinge.

Take my last breathe and heartbeat away—
choose—my own demise in a watery grave—
consume by the ocean, devour by sharks—
effortless to the sea, or flying high—high
Above The Spirit Tree

Poem
Category: Peace

When the Wind Blows Hate
by
Beatrice Vasser

Prejudice circulates thru the breeze
as evil languages soar relentlessly in air,
inhales deep antagonist breathes—
consumes the minds and intoxicates the souls
in a storm of racial rhetoric—out of control.

Rage stocks anger
Murder occurs
Gun kills—innocent people die.
Purity is white,
Colored emanates hate.

Diversity alarms the bigots, they say,
Go back to where you come from—tell this
to Indians, the winds track them to reservations.
America is not white again, never was, since 1619.
A country is great off the backs of slaves.

Reverse the wind,
blow it with truth not terror.
a breath of air—pure
a color without—fear
"love—not hate."

P—E—A—C—E

Poem
Category: Healing

I Use My Hands
by
Beatrice Vasser

When you clench your fist no one can put anything in your hand.
—Alex Haley
To govern my life—
I spread the fingers for the span
encircles the arms for warmth and care
points the pinky to guide my directions
opens my palm to caress the pleasures
flex the fingers, to grab, to hold—
the nails to scratch and calm the itch
between each finger a breath of air.
Clinches the fist to protect and defend
to hold the cycles of life within.
Oh! oh these mighty hands

Prayer
Category: Healing

Love of Self Radiates
by
William Thiele

All my life I focused on loving others
I was raised that way so that it came natural
But I was never taught boundaried love

So boundless love flowed forth
over and over
until I became very tired

My soul was weary from too much giving
and not enough receiving
because I did not know love of self is blessed

After the crash
after realizing I just couldn't keep going
at that old pace,
my soul rose up
delight began to ebb back into my cracks and crevices
joy surprised me
and my inner life became important

Now the first morning priority is filling the inner reservoir
and then I keep Sourcing during the day
and sometimes I Source again in the evening
I try to Source while I serve
I honor the Great Walkaway from service when needed
And I seek to live on the liminal threshold

Now the Source is my daily True Home
Now love of self radiates

***

Dr. William Thiele has over the years challenged me to enjoy the quiet, gentle, contemplative nature of life. He is the founder of the School for Contemplative Living. He is the author of the book *Monks in the World: Seeking God in a Frantic Culture*. He also has the *A Contemplative Path* podcast on iTunes and blog on Wordpress.com.

Reflections: Chapter 6

As a country and as a world, we had been focusing on the economy and praying for a cure for COVID-19. On May 26, 2020, the world watched in horror as Police Officer Derek Chauvin killed George Floyd, who was pleading, "I can't breathe!" and crying out for his momma.

1. Where were you physically, emotionally, and spiritually on May 26, 2020?

2. Today's Date:

Where are you physically, emotionally, and spiritually today?

3. Did any of the poems speak to you? Which ones and why?

4. Black, Brown, and some other simpatico people are sick and tired of the hatred, racism, negativity, and chaos. How do you feel? Do you see any hope? Where is God?

5. What do you do when something chaotic happens in your life? Please continue to pray for the protestors and the police. Pray for an end to the injustices that exist in these troubled times.

Read Ecclesiastes 3:1–8. What's going on?

Contemplating life

CHAPTER 7

Wearing Hats

In July, living through the midst of it all, I attended a hat-wearing virtual fundraiser party sponsored by my Zeta sorority sister and mentor Dr. Rosalind Hale. She was at her home in Alabama, and I was at my home in Louisiana. Other attendees were at their homes, but we were at the party. We had a good time and money was raised. It was an opportunity for me to stay connected to wearing my hats. Many people were doing what we needed to do to weather and live through the pandemic storms. People were working virtually from their homes, finding ways to stay connected to each other, and even having some fun. People were also discovering that virtually we could be in more than one place at a time.

Tisha Orphe Sonnier wearing and walking that hat

Prayer

Wearing Hats
by
Dr. Rosalind Hale

Phase 1: Colors
A hat does more than
Protect one's head from the sun,
Wind, rain, sleet and snow.

It gives meaning to
Our true personalities,
Good and sometimes bad.

Hurt and sometimes sad;
Happy, indifferent
or
Even fun loving.

Most feelings observed
Easily are grief with black
And joy with bright colors.

Everyone knows
My fav'rite is royal blue.
True color of joy.

Dr. Rosalind Pijeaux Hale wearing her favorite color, royal blue

Carlus Anthony Olivier and granddaughters
Bailey Jh'nae Olivier
Madisyn Jolie Olivier
(Niece and great-great-nieces)
Hat wearing across the generations

Phase 2: Styles
What style is your hat?
Cap, Brim, tam, or wide each day.
What does it tell us?

Caps over the head.
Could mean a bad hair day?
Maybe bad weather

Brims show lots of hair.
New styles to exhibit now.
Will anyone notice?

Tams tilt this way or
That depending on your focus.
Impress on left or right.

Wide can mean wonder.
See me or not, try your best.
Waiting for someone.

A hat that is high
Implies look up quickly or
You may not see me.

What style are you?
Does your style change with your mood?
Mine does, can you tell?

Left to right:
Ashley Orphe, Kizzie Orphe, Monica Tyler Batiste, Aunt Martha, Sharika Batiste Hawkins, Carlus Anthony Olivier
(Some of the nieces)
Tisha Orphe Bridal Shower 2014

Aunt Clara Tyler Jean Batiste and Shawntae Batiste
Passing on the tradition

Shawntae Batiste, Aunt Rev. Martha, Sharika Batiste Hawkins
Passing on the tradition

Top photo: Kizzie Orphe, Sharika Hawkins,
Carlus Olivier
Bottom Photo, front to back: Aunt Martha, Kizzie Orphe, Khalon Toussant,
Kendrick Toussant Jr., Jayden Collins, and Jaylen Collins
(Some of the nieces and nephews with some of the hat wearers)

Phase 3: Sizes and Textures

Hats come in many
Sizes and textures to say
Something about us.

Wide, high, rough show strength,
Domineering over all
Around the wearer

Narrow means kindness,
Happiness, sincerity,
Loving all people.

Smooth and soft mean joy.
Always smiling, never sad.
Fun to be around.

Imagine a world
Without hats to wear each day.
Could you handle it?

Wanda Porter Johnson and daughters Delana and Dailee Johnson passing on the tradition

***

Wanda Johnson and her family are members of the Louisiana Avenue United Methodist Church in Lafayette, Louisiana. She and her family continue to work with her childhood church, Mallalieu United Methodist Church, where we served in many ministries together. Wanda Johnson is a community leader in St. Martinville. She is a justice of the peace.

Tisha Orphe Sonnier Family
Left to right: Ashley Orphe, Richard Sonnier, Tisha Orphe Sonnier, Jaylen Collins, and Jayden Collins wearing hats and enjoying the holidays together

Friends have prayed for and covered me in prayer. I have covered friends in my prayers. We inspire each other. We cheer each other on!

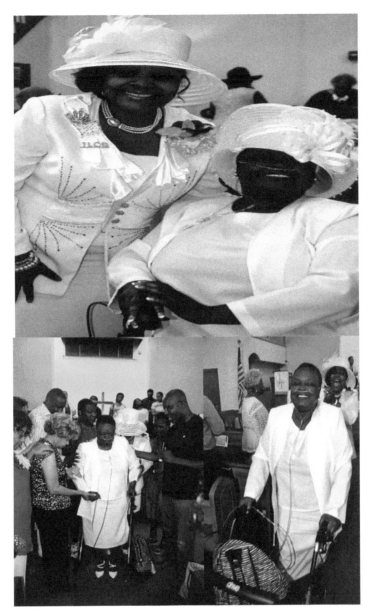

Friends prayed for me
Celebrating the conclusion of 33 years of ministry
April 2017

Rev. Trina Williams is one of my daughters in the ministry. I am her mentor and she is my mentee. She and her family are family and friends. Rev. Trina Williams is the pastor of Mount Zion United Methodist Church in Clinton, Louisiana, and St. Paul United Methodist Church in Ethel, Louisiana. She is also the state program coordinator for the Louisiana Healthy Homes and Childhood Lead Poisoning Prevention Program.

I appreciate all the friends who pray for me.

***

Linda and Rosalind are my forever friends. Rosalind James Griffin and I are not only friends, but we are also cousins and sisters in Christ. Rosalind is a praying woman of God. We grew up in farm families, where we learned the value of hard work, family, and knowing God. Her father was my godfather. Rosalind raised her family in our hometown and is a private home nurse.

Wearing hats for any occasion and any outfit

Top photo: Forever friends—Linda Perrodin Mallery, Rev. Martha, and Rosalind James Griffin
Lower photo: Rev. Martha and Nina Nurridin Hodges

***

Nina is my interfaith Muslim friend and sister. One day during Black History Month, Nina sent me a note. It read,

> Girl, I wore this at the Marrero Street Center
> If Rev can wear her Royal Purple hat with Her African attire,
> I can do so with my red and gold.

Yes indeed!
February 2020

For me, the elders are always watching over us, covering us. We remember all our elders. Some are shown in the following picture.

Top photo, standing from left to right: second person, Stella Orphe Batiste (my sister)
Sitting: Paul J. Batiste Sr. and Almeda R. Batiste (Stella's-in-laws)
Lower photo, from left to right: Leo Orphe (my uncle) and Castille Orphe (my aunt
and godmother), Dolores (*sitting*) and Joseph Orphe (my parents)
Remembering some of our deceased elders. May they rest in peace!

We honor our elders who are still among us.
Top photo: William "Flee" Batiste (my brother-in-law) and his brother Donald Batiste and wife, Priscilla Batiste
Lower photo: Della Francis Orphe (my only living aunt)

The haiku poem about hats reminds us that hats come in different styles, sizes, and colors and have different purposes, including covering us. Work hats and caps are yet another type of hat. We pray and then we get off our knees and work, putting our faith in God into action.

In the midst of the COVID pandemic, hurricanes left a trail of destruction in different areas of the southern coast. One area was the Lake Charles, Louisiana, area. Practicing social distancing to prevent the spread of the virus, people responded to people in need. The Orphe Generational Foundation (OGF), Mallalieu UMC, and the Louisiana Ave UMC responded by putting our beliefs into action.

Working hats
Rev. Robert Johnson, pastor of the Ave Church, and Ashley Orphe, OGF board president, worked together to load the truck with supplies.

Faith in Action
United Methodist Church Campaign—"PUTTING BELIEFS INTO ACTION-THAT'S CHURCH." *Wearing masks*, Rev. Martha with Ashley Orphe, OGF president, as she shopped for cleaning supplies.

Picture
taken
2016
No Mask
Required

Mallalieu United Methodist Church
Rev. Valla Johnson and Rev. Martha

Supplies from Mallalieu UMC—pastor, Rev. Valla Johnson—were also loaded into the truck. The truck was driven to the Lake Charles, Louisiana, area. We are covered by hats and prayers as we do the work of God.

The scripture in Hebrews 4:16 (NRSV) says, "Let us therefore approach the throne of grace with boldness, so that we may receive mercy and find grace to help in time of need."

Reflections: Chapter 7

1. In 2020, were you able to find new and innovative ways to have some fun with family and friends while social distancing and wearing a mask?

2. Today's Date:

How are you safely connecting with others?

3. In 2020, were you able to serve God through serving others? How? When?

How did serving others make you feel?

Prayer
Wednesday Prayer Call, July 15, 2020, 12:15 p.m.

COVID-19: Rise in Cases
Impact upon the Black and Brown Communities
by
Rev. Martha Orphe

Gospel songwriter and singer, Kirk Franklin, sings the song, "My world needs you right now." Lord God Almighty, we are praying to you from different parts of the world and our world needs you right now more than our words can express.

This Covid-19 Virus continues to darken our world and our nation. The spread of the virus is on the rise again. Forgive us for not listening and that some of our own behavior/misbehavior have given this enemy yet another foot hold on us. Lord, when will we learn?

Lord, many of us as African Americans and other People of Color feel like we have gotten more than our fair-share of this virus. And we are asking you Lord, **why when there is a Pandemic for the world, it is a Super Pandemic for People of Color, why when it is bad for all, it is worst for People of Color.**

Lord we are praying we get a Break from this Virus. We are praying we catch a break. We don't want harm, hurt or danger to go to anyone else because we know what it feels like but we are asking for a Break. We want the best health care and the best health and economic environments just like everybody else. But Lord help us to acknowledge we must take care of ourselves **Lord, we want a different experience, a different story, a different way of life, a life that does not include being at the brunt of illnesses and sickness at a higher rate than others**. Lord, we need you right now.

Lord, God, we have spoken our minds, we have said our peace, we have made our petitions known and we have shared the desires of our hearts but now O God we do ask that your will be done but know our world, we need you right now. Amen.

CHAPTER 8

Corona Season
Protest Season
Hurricane Season

During the summer months, more COVID-19 testing became available. It was corona season. It was protest season. On the West Coast, it was wildfire season, and in the southern coastal states, it was an unprecedented hurricane season of five hurricanes leaving much emotional, financial, and property damage. The pandemic continued, and the social and political unrest and racial divide continued in the United States. Now the natural disasters were also added to our prayers.

Also during these summer months, there were protests all around the country and the world. A peaceful protest was held at the courthouse in St. Martinville, Louisiana, on Saturday, July 18, 2020. The protest was organized by a St. Martinville native, a twenty-two-year-old who was passionate for justice, Sarah Pierre. Sarah entered as a law student at Ole Miss in Oxford, Mississippi, in the fall 2020. Every day for a week before the protest, Sarah would walk around the courthouse and surrounding area and pray. The day before this peaceful protest, two civil rights leaders, John Lewis and Rev. C. T. Vivian, passed away. They worked tirelessly for justice. People came out and showed support for unity and Black Lives Matter at the peaceful protest in St. Martinville, as they did around the world. A moment of silence was held in memory of Lewis and Vivian followed by calls for justice and unity. Our hearts were heavy, but we knew the work of justice must go on.

Prayer
Wednesday Prayer Call, July 29, 2020

What's Going On?
by
Rev. Martha Orphe

Most merciful and Gracious God we have gathered to pray to you. Lord, before we ask you for anything we want to praise your Holy Name. Lord God, we want to thank you for who you are. You are God and you are God all by yourself. We thank you God for what you do, what you have done, and what you are doing and what you will be doing in this world, in our nation, in our state, in our cities, in our towns and in our lives.

Lord, our long hard working civil rights activists, John Lewis and C. T. Vivian, have gone on to glory. In the midst of all this death, killings, racism, injustices, some of our leaders are gone. We thank you for their lives of leadership and service. Lord, give us strength and courage to get into some "Good Trouble" as we continue the work for justice and peace.

Lord, we are asking, is this really happening? We are raising the question that singers, activists, preachers, teachers, mothers, and fathers have been and continue to ask— "What's going on?"

What's going on with the rise and fall of the COVID-19 virus cases?

What's going on with people not wanting to wear a mask to ensure the health of the community?

What's going on with these stimulus checks?

What's going on with evicting people from their homes in the midst of a Pandemic?

Lord, what's going on with In-Person Classroom teaching and virtual classrooms?

What's going on in Portland, in Chicago, in Florida, in New Orleans?

What's going on with the President of these not so united United States?

Lord God Almighty, what is going on?

Each week we gather to pray and each week we have questions. Each week we have yet more concerns and even anger. Lord, help us this week to once again experience your peace and your power and your presence.

Calm us Lord like only you can do. Empower us to what we can do like only you can do. Let us experience your presence in the atmosphere around us. Let us experience your peace, power and presence to make it to tomorrow, to make it to next week. Help us to be strong and courageous so we can do the work we must do in the midst all that is going on. Lord, we believe you will be with us, for the Bible tells us that you are with us. We thank you Lord Jesus because we do not want to get into any "Good Trouble" without you.

Lord God, hear our hearts as we ask questions, we are seeking understanding and direction. So we ask questions and we pray.

Lord, we ask questions but Lord we pray. We pray for those who have lost loved ones to the virus. We pray for recovery for those who are suffering from the virus. We pray for all the front line workers. Lord we pray for the wearing of masks and other guidelines that we need to follow in this Pandemic in order to have the number of cases go down. Lord God we don't want to go backwards. We want to go forward into the future you have for us. Lord, we don't know what the future holds, but we know who holds the future. You O God Almighty hold our future.

Lord, we ask questions but we pray. There are many in our government at all levels who are making decisions about our future. We pray for Governor John Bel Edwards as he guides in the State of Louisiana and calls us to prayer and fasting. Lord, we pray for Mayor LaToya Cantrell as she leads the city of New Orleans. Lord, we pray for the Governors and Mayors of the states, cities, towns, throughout this nation. We pray for leaders around the world. Guide their feet, their minds and their hearts to create a better life for all of us.

Guide our feet, our minds and our hearts to make a difference and make the change we believe you want us to be and do! We thank you Lord God. We thank you that even if we don't know all of what's going on, we know you know what's going on. And so we continue to pray. We trust you, O Lord. Amen and Amen.

Prayer

A Litany in Tribute to
The Honorable John R. Lewis

Good Trouble
by
Rev. Clifton C. Conrad Sr.

Leader: In the Gospel of John, chapter 2, we find Jesus upending the tables of the money changers.

People: **Jesus knew how to get into "Good Trouble!"**

Leader: In the Gospel of Matthew, chapter 14, John the Baptist gets thrown into jail after confronting King Herod over his affair with his brother's wife.

People: **John the Baptist knew how to get into "Good Trouble!"**

Leader: In 1 Kings, chapter 19, Elijah is sent running from Jezebel after his confrontation with the priests of Baal and Astarte on Mt. Carmel.

People: **Elijah knew how to get into "Good Trouble!"**

Leader: In Acts, chapter 16, Paul and Silas get thrown into jail for casting out a demon.

People: **Paul and Silas knew how to get into "Good Trouble!"**

Leader: In Daniel, chapter 3, Shadrach, Meshach and Abednego were thrown into the fiery furnace for refusing to bow to the Nebuchadnezzar's idol.

People: **Shadrach, Meshach and Abednego knew how to get into "Good Trouble!"**

All: Lord, Your word speaks of those who were willing to get into "Good Trouble," on your behalf. Give us the boldness, courage and desire to seek your justice; speak Your Word; and witness to our faith in you. **Lord, be with us as we seek to get into "Good Trouble!"** Amen!

 Kimberly PoppasMom Dauterive is with **Sarah Pierre.**
Jul 18, 2020 · 🌐   •••

What an amazing day! Peaceful protest and gathering to take steps towards unification and solidarity in St. Martinville. I'm so proud of you Sarah! St. Martinville, this is just the beginning 🙌🙌🙌🙌

🔵 KLFY NEWS 10 · 1 MIN READ
Peacefull rally calls on unification in St. Martinville

Shown masked in picture, seated: Rev. Martha, Tisha Orphe Sonnier, Wanda Porter Johnson, and Ashley Orphe
Photo credit: KFLY News Station, Lafayette, Louisiana

Reflection

That Town
by
Linda Perrodin Mallery

I'm from that town ... you know it well
The one that scheduled a class reunion for "Whites Only"
And had the audacity to post it on Facebook!
Of course, the post went viral

Sometimes I think there's hope for my hometown
The one I left behind at 18
But then sometimes I think
The more things change, the more they remain the same
Who knows?
Only time will tell

Reflections: Chapter 8

The political climate temperature of the country continued to rise. The United States has become a divided nation.

1. What is going on? What are your thoughts on our past and current state of affairs?

2. Where was God? Did you seek God in prayer? Who were you covering in prayer? Who covered you in prayer?

3. Did your prayer time increase, decrease, or perhaps not exist?

CHAPTER 9

So Many People Are Dying

Prayer
Wednesday Prayer Call, August 12, 2020

For Everything There Is a Season
by
Rev. Martha Orphe
Ecclesiastes 3:1–8

Gracious God, the scriptures tell us there is a season and a time for everything, every activity under the sun.

Lord, today many of us are feeling like everything that can happen under the sun, is happening under the sun to us. Lord, we thank you for all the good things but we know there will also be the not so good things, the bad and the ugly things in this life.

Remind us that no matter what is happening, no matter what thing we are experiencing, no matter what season we are living in, You O God, you are with us. You are with us with the Cancer, in the Fires, the divorce, in the storm, the cheating spouse, in the Social and Racial Unrest, the unemployment, the Covid-19 Virus. You O God have not abandoned us. **We are not alone. You are with us**.

Even in the time of death and dying you are with us. So we pray for those who are in the **season in the time of grief and sorrow**. We pray for those who are mourning the death of their loved ones. We pray for your presence with them. Bless those in the Mourning Season.

Lord God we pray for those in the **season of Healing**. We pray for those who are sick from the Covid-19 Virus and other sickness and diseases. Heal them in this Season of Healing.

Lord God we pray for all of us in this Pandemic as we have been unable to embrace one another unable to care for our sick loved ones in hospitals, in nursing home even embrace those quarantined shut up in their homes as we are separated and isolated one from another in this **Season of Refraining from Embracing**. Lord as we **refrain from physically** embracing each other help us to embrace you more and more spiritually. Help us to **embrace spending quiet time praying and listening to you O God.**

Lord, we pray our government officials at every level will embrace listening to you. Let them be still and know you are God. O lord let us be in a season of silence where we can hear your still small voice and then O lord **let us be in the season to speak up and say thus says the Lord.** Let us speak up and speak out that our children's lives matter, our teacher's lives matter, as schools are opening all around this country.

Almighty God your Word reminds us that **there is a time and a season for war and the season of Hate. Lord, some of us feel like we have been living in the season, in the time of hate, all our lives.** Lord help us to bring about the season, the time to tear down the hate, to dismantle the racism, and the sexism, tear down all the "isms" and injustices in this world. But Lord we know that tearing down can and often does lead to the time of war. War of words, War of Armies, War of Spiritual Warfare. Lord you are with us even in these difficult times. You are our shield and rock. We acknowledge this time of confusion, conflict and war and we proclaim boldly that we will fight and we will win because if you O God are with us, who can be against us and who can even think they can win. Lord help us in this season and time of war against our enemy the Covid-19 virus. We know we cannot fight this battle alone. Precious Lord, fight our battle, for the battle is not ours but this battle is the Lord's battle. Release your cure and take this evil away from us, God Almighty.

Lord God some of us **feel we have not been in the season, in the time of joy and laughter and dancing for a long time.** We have been shut up in our homes for months but lord help us to laugh and to sing and dance for you as we give you all the praise, glory and honor, for we are alive and we are healthy. Help us to be in the season and time of building and mending broken hearts and broken relationships, broken structures and broken systems to be about peace in the Ultimate seasons of love and perfect peace with you.

Yes Lord there is a season and a time for everything under the sun. Help us to know you are with us in every season no matter what the thing is and no matter what the time may come in our lives. You are with us! We are not alone! Amen.

***

On August 28, 2020, Chadwick Boseman, "the Black Panther," died. If our young children were not experiencing the heaviness of the deaths of George Floyd and others, the death of the Black Panther hit home—and not just for the children. The Black Panther had brought so many of us to a place where African Black people did not experience colonization, slavery, and racism as a part of their history. Although a movie, it gave so much hope, beyond hope.

Prayer

A Lament
by
Rev. Martha Orphe

Lord, Our Black Panther has died. Our young Black Leader has died. Lord we thank you for the amazing work on and off screen of young Chadwick Boseman. May we remember his leadership forever! He did his work. May his soul rest in power. Help us to do our work of justice and peace, Jesus, Lord of Lords, and king of kings. Amen.

***

People were dying every day in our personal and national lives. As if we did not have enough to deal with living through COVID-19, Black people continued to suffer the injustices, the brutalities, and the violence. Some describe it as Black people being in a bereavement crisis, grieving, lamenting. Will it ever stop? We prayed.

Our prayers also thanked God for the good things that were happening in our lives, but the challenges made this 2020 year a year like no other, and thus we knew we had to be covered by prayer. We prayed for our families, our friends, our neighbors, our coworkers, our communities, our states, our country, our government leaders at all levels. We prayed for our enemies.

I covered others in my prayers and always appreciate others covering me in prayer. I really appreciated the prayers the day I received the phone call that my adoptive church daughter, Dr. Keion Davis Parker, was on a ventilator at a hospital in New Orleans. I wanted to go to her, but that was not possible because of hospital restrictions and my high-risk health condition. I called and prayed with Keion.

I needed prayer that day. I needed to be covered in prayer. The entire family needed to be covered in prayer. I am so grateful that on September 8, the family gathered around Keion, and I prayed on the phone with her, with them, before literally this beautiful, smart, and fun-loving forty-two-year-old lead pharmacist, wife, mother of two children, daughter, and friend left her earthly home.

During the presidential debates, we, like so many others in the world, understood the words of Presidential Candidate Joe Biden, "the empty chairs at dining tables."

Top photo: Keion *(blue dress center)* and Family
Lower Photo: Left, Dr. Keion Davis Parker
August 18, 1978–September 8, 2020
Right, Nedra Davis Melancon
August 20, 1954—December 30, 2012

The next day, September 9, 2020, I prayed with my Wednesday prayer group. I could not keep the tears back, so I knew I needed to share what was happening. I said, "I don't know about all of you, but this day, like so many other days, I need some help. Yesterday, my forty-two-year-old adoptive daughter lost her battle with stage 4 pancreatic cancer. She left behind a husband, a son in college, and a daughter in first grade. We thank God for her life although we say it was short. On days like today, those of us who are still on this earth need help to keep us going. We need help from God living through everything we are experiencing."

I don't know about others, but for me, in 2020, it felt like death was all around us more than ever before—death from COVID-19, death from cancer, and death from natural causes. We pray people will live their lives on earth in ways that when death comes, they can live their lives in heaven.

We wear different hats on earth—for example, mother hat, wife hat, husband hat, community worker hat, provider hat, and so on. The hope is we will exchange our hats for a crown and hear the Lord say to us, "well done, good and faithful servant." (Matthew 25:23). The gospel song, "When the Battle's Over, I Shall Wear a Crown" says,

> I shall wear a crown
> I shall wear a crown
> When it's all over
> When it's all over
> I'm going to put on my robe
> Tell the story how I made it over
> Soon as I get home."[2]

Keion is home. She has exchanged her hats for a crown. She can put on her robe, and she can tell the story of how she made it over. I believe Keion is living her life in heaven with her mother, Nedra, and other family members and friends. Rest in peace.

We needed some peace in our lives. We needed some peace in our country.

We prayed, how much more, Lord? How much?

> We prayed in honor of the life and work of
> Supreme Court Justice
> Ruth Bader Ginsburg
> March 15, 1933–September 18, 2020
> Rest in peace.

Prayer
Wednesday Prayer Call, September 23, 2020

Lord God, We Pray the Famous Serenity Prayer
by
Rev. Martha Orphe

"God, grant me the serenity to accept the things I cannot change, the courage to change the things I can, and the wisdom to know the difference."

Lord, we pray for serenity. Lord we are living in situations we never thought or imagined we would be living in. But Lord we are living through this crazy year 2020. These are such stressful times. It disturbs our spirits that over 200,000 people in the United States have died from COVID-19. Lord, and that is not including all the other people who are dying from other things. Lord, our spirits have been grieving and lamenting, O God. In the midst of it all grant us serenity, grant us peace. We seek your peace and comfort. For

---

2. John Avery Lomax, "When the Battle's Over, I Shall Wear a Crown," 1940.

many of us, our hearts are saddened by the death of Supreme Court Justice Ruth Bader Ginsburg. We pray for her family. May she rest in peace from this earthly work for justice! We thank you for her life and for her work. Lord, help us continue the good work that she and so many others have started.

Lord, we pray for the decisions that will be made to fill her Supreme Court vacancy.

Lord, we pray for Breonna Taylor's family as decisions are being made about her death in the next few weeks. Lord, let there be justice.

Lord, we continue to pray for all who are affected by the fires, tropical storms, and hurricanes. Even in this time of social distancing, wearing masks, etc., give us vision of how we can help our hurting brothers and sisters

Lord, as the days are quickly nearing for the elections, we are experiencing the divide and tension in this country. We pray your will be done and we ask you to give us the serenity to accept what we cannot change. But Lord we know what we cannot change you can change. You have all power and might. But help us to have peace with what you do and what is done.

Lord, this prayer reminds us to pray for courage to do the things we can do, to change the things we can change. Help us to speak up and to speak out against injustices, racism, sexism, and police brutality. Help us to work to change laws and policies. Help us to vote to change leaders and officials so that peace and justice can reign. Lord, help us to have faith and confidence.

Lord we know we see life through our own experiences and our own eyes. Sometimes as human beings we want to change things based solely on how we see things, how it feels to us, how it benefits us with little or no regard to how it will affect others. Lord, when Solomon in the Bible had the opportunity to ask you for anything, anything he could want, he asked you to give him wisdom. Lord, there are a lot of things we can ask you for today, but help us to ask you for wisdom.

Give us wisdom for the living of each hour and the living for each day. Grant us wisdom to know what we cannot change and know what we can change and know the difference. *Hear our prayer, Lord. Amen and Amen.*

Prayer

A Prayer for Guidance
by
Stefanie Dandy Cole

Our Father Who Art in Heaven, lead us and guide us on this journey called life. Take the coals off of our eyes so that we can see your footprints before us and take the wax out of our ears so we can hear your voice clearly when you speak to us. Let not our hearts be hardened to change, love, wisdom, knowledge and understanding.

I pray that we study the Word of God more, love each other more and spread the gospel of Jesus Christ on a daily basis so souls will be saved to enter into the Kingdom of Heaven in the Mighty Name of Jesus Amen!

I want to thank you Lord for your new mercies every day! For love, grace, joy, food, shelter, water, good health and that is just to name a few! Lord if I had ten thousand tongues I will praise you with every last one!!! You deserve all the glory and honor because you are Alpha and Omega (the beginning and the end), Jehovah Jireh (The Lord our Provider)!!! Hallelujah thank you Jesus!!!

Stephanie Dandy Cole "Saints Fans" Family

***

Stephanie Dandy Cole has a strong faith in God, and we enjoy being sisters in Christ. Since she was a teenager, her favorite scripture has been "I can do all things through Christ who strengthens me!" (Philippians 4:13). We have made a lot of things happen as sorority sisters. Stephanie graduated from Langston University in Tulsa, Oklahoma, and is a teacher. She and her husband are parents to four boys. She enjoys helping others and spending time with her family, especially being Saints fans.

Reflections: Chapter 9

We found ourselves living through month after month of 2020, and people continued to die of COVID-19. We wondered if it was ever going to stop.

1. How did you respond to the feelings of despair that were so pervasive as we began to approach the end of the year?

2. Did any of the prayers and poems speak to you? Which ones? Why?

3. Did you seek God in prayer? Who were you covering in prayer?

Who was covering you in prayer?

Read Ecclesiastes 3:1–8.

CHAPTER 10

School Openings?

We were approaching the return to school. Would schools be in-person or virtual? How would we keep our children, teachers, and school workers safe in the pandemic? There was no break in sight.

Schools trained teachers. Many teachers were converted into tech-savvy leaders who could handle the electronic classrooms, assignments, grading, reporting, and whatever was specifically needed to provide virtual learning or in-person learning. In many cases, the transition happened very quickly. In the education systems, some learned just how quickly we can make changes, just how quickly we can adjust.

Prayer
Wednesday Prayer Call, August 26, 2020

I Pray for Real
by
Rev. Orphe

Many times I am led to pray from an old church hymn. This prayer included words from two young Gospel Singers Peter Cottontail and Chance the Rapper as they reached out to the younger generations.

Lord, we pray for all involved in the return to schools, the children, the students, the teachers, the administrators, the school staff, the bus drivers, etc.

In the midst of this Pandemic, we pray for the opening of schools. Lord, we want our children to get their education, but we also want everybody to be safe from the virus. Lord, help us to really pray and pray for real as **Peter Cottontail** and **Chance the Rapper** also pray for real with these words:

> So I pray for the good days, I pray for bad days
> I pray for my report card, like, **"stay away bad grades"**

Go away bad vibes, **I pray for my classmates**
I pray that when they walk in, it won't be their last day
I pray for real, I pray for real
I talk to God, then I wait for real
I pray for fun, **I pray for real**
I pray for ya'll, I pray for ya'll[3]

Lord, God, we are praying for real today. We are praying for everybody. Hear us as we pray.

Poem

Rest Assure
by
Mrs. Charity Turpeau, MEd

-**Decisions and adjustment** have to be made **from a math educator's point of view**
To some it seems like many and to others it seems like a few.

-**Math**
now mask

-6 feet
now **6 deep**

-Yo-Kid
now **Covid**

-Decontextualize
now when to hand **sanitize**

-Fraction of stripes
now locating **Clorox wipes**

-Line segments and rays
now controlling the amount of **Lysol sprays**

-Measuring angles greater than 95
now scanning **forehead fevers** above 99

-Absolute values
now **social distance** in hallway travels

---

3.   Peter CottonTale, "Pray For Real," track 13 on *CATCH*, RCM, 2020.

-Mode, average, and mean
now how long and when to **quarantine**

-However, with prayer, correct steps, and faces covered
homes, schools, and soon the world will be on the road to recover

-It doesn't matter if in Phase one or two
now let us just do what we are asked to do

-So my fellow 20–21 educators, parents, and community members this is now our new unique situation
but *Rest Assure* that in my class your child will be welcomed, respected, and delivered a world class education.

July/2020

Poem

A Teacher's Morning Prayer
by
Mary Hogan Carter

Heavenly Father,
Before I begin my work today,
I need to take a moment to pray.
I'm asking you Father to order my steps and be my guide,
I am always at my best with you by my side.
I pray that you give me the knowledge that I will need;
To show these young people how to succeed.
Help me to teach them what they need to know,
And the strength to tell some, which path they should go.
Please keep me in perfect peace, no matter what this day may bring,
Father God, I give you praise, glory and honor for everything.
In Jesus Name I pray. Amen.

***

President Mary Hogan Carter is the fierce leader of the Zeta Phi Beta Sorority, Inc., Alpha Gamma Zeta Chapter-New Orleans. She leads with the humility and strength of a Christian woman. For thirty-five years, she has been a math teacher, coach, and mentor at Jefferson High School in Harvey, Louisiana. She was named the 2020 teacher of the year. She is a faithful member of St. Joseph Missionary Baptist Church in Marrero, Louisiana.

Poem

A Coke Zero for a Hero
by
Mrs. Charity (Turp) Turpeau, MEd

You are doing your job wonderfully and superb
While others can only wait, pray, sit, and observe

Sip the soda of your choice filled with lots of bubbles
In hopes to decrease or erase any stress, or overwhelming troubles

Untwist the top, hear the sound, and enjoy the feel of the fizz
Knowing you are helping someone because you are a blessed smart whiz

As you finish this drink let out a big sigh and a soft burp
Knowing that your #1 fan is the creator of your heart under your shirt

So to keep you healthy and wealthy
Enjoy *A Coke Zero* because you are *A Hero*

Feb/2020

Reflections: Chapter 10

1. Listen to the full song, "Pray for Real," by Chance the Rapper and Peter Cotton Tale. What are your thoughts?

2. Educating our children in America is important. Educating our children in the midst of a health pandemic is challenging. Education and safety are both equally important. How do we keep students, teachers, and all other school workers safe?

3. What do you think worked in 2020, and what do you think did not work?

We thank all our frontline workers, teachers, and all other school workers for your service.

Prayer

Prayer for the Government
by
Mary Hogan Carter

Our Father and our God, the creator of heaven and earth; I come to you as humbly and submissively as I know how, acknowledging that you are God and God all by yourself. You are the giver and sustainer of life, you hear all, see all, you know all and you can do all things but fail. I give you all the honor, praise and glory and I say Hallelujah to your name. Father I ask that you forgive us all for our sins and help us to make everything that we do be pleasing in your sight. I would like to thank you Lord for your grace, mercy, your everlasting love, and most of all for your son Jesus Christ whom you sacrificed for those of us here on earth.

Father, I lay before your throne of grace, our government. You ordained government to keep order in the world; but that doesn't always happen. So, I ask that you bless our nation through Godly leaders. In your word it says we should pray for all men and also for Kings and all that are in authority; so that we, the children of God, may lead a quiet and peaceable life in all godliness and honesty. I am asking right now God that you touch the hearts of all who are in authority; all officials that are elected or appointed to serve your people. I pray that they receive the wisdom of God and act in obedience to your Word. Help them Lord to know you and see your presence in the work they do.

I pray that all who are in authority make no decisions that will bring harm to your children in any way. Reveal your perfect will Lord to our leaders. I pray that the members of the Senate and the House of Representatives find your peace and direction. A house divided against itself cannot stand, so I pray for them to be unified in righteousness for the sake of our nation. Guide the tongues of all leaders so that they can speak respectfully and with humility to one another. Help them to show Christ-like love in everything they do. Father, I pray for all the leaders of churches open in your name. Strengthen them Lord, crown their heads with wisdom and knowledge, and put a hedge of protection around them as they continue to lead and guide your people. Thank you Lord for always loving us and never forsaking us. I pray this prayer in the name of our Lord and Savior Jesus Christ. Amen

CHAPTER 11

Debates, Voting, Elections

There was no break. The COVID-19 pandemic was in the middle of the United States' presidential election. The United States was divided. The divide in the racial and political climate of the country was at a level like many of us had never before. The hatred, the intimidation tactics, and the violence against people of color had been on the rise throughout the year.

Reflection
Wednesday Prayer Call, September 30, 2020

Stand Back, Stand By
by
Rev. Martha Orphe

Scripture Text:

"For God has not given us the spirit of fear, but of Power and of Love and of a Sound Mind." (2 Timothy 1:7 NKJV)

The world witnessed the disastrous Presidential Debate last night, September 29th. I was following friends on Facebook and many of the messages were:

We need the Lord.

If we've ever needed the Lord before, we sure do need Him now!

Help! Our country is in trouble!

Yes, our country is in trouble. When President Donald Trump said he wants the Proud Boys White Supremacist Group to "Stand Back and Stand By" that sounded like that could be a threat, some kind of intimidation and fear tactic.

For many these words may still be ringing in our ears and causing us to be in some kind of way in our feelings.

Today I remind us Sorority Sisters that God has not given us a Spirit of Cowardice, a Spirit of Fear, but of Power and of Love and of a Sound Mind!

These are some dark and frightening days. There are 34 days left before November 3rd. But we will not fear! We will be Powerfully Strong and we will use our Sound Minds to make decisions and take actions at the polls. And we will give witness to the Love of God.

Let us pray:

Lord, God Almighty, if ever we needed the Lord before, we sure do need you now O Lord. Just when we thought it could not get worse, it is getting worse. Remind us O Lord that you have not given us a spirit of fear. We do not have to fear anything, we do not need to fear anybody. Lord, bind the spirit of fear in the name and Blood of Jesus. The scriptures tell us, I shall not fear the arrow by day, nor shall I fear the terror by night. We know the God who governs Angel Armies has set encampments around me, whom shall I fear? Though I walk through the valley of death, I will fear no evil.

Lord, there is a lot of evil in the world, but we need not fear. We must stand up to evil with the power of God.

Help us to live as your witnesses in this land when others try to intimidate us, even tell us to go back to where we've come from. Go back to Africa.

Many have sung the song, "This land is your land"

This land is your land, this land is my land.

This land was made for you and me.

Lord, there are white supremacist and racist people who think this land is only their land and is not for others. They try to demean us. They do not value us as brother and sister, or see us as human beings, let alone a child of God ... We pray for their lack of understanding that this land is for all of us. Lord we pray for their refusal to understand that you, O God, you value us. We are all your children, red, yellow, black, brown and white and we are all precious in your sight. So, Lord, we are praying for all of us in this land.

Lord, we pray for the approaching elections. Lord, we pray for all those who believe their vote doesn't count. Help them to understand they matter and their vote matters to help make the world better for all of us. As the elections are approaching, we have many thoughts and emotions. Help us to use our sound minds, our emotions, and our feet and get ourselves and others to the ballot boxes. We are not afraid. Let us show the world what your Spirit of Power and Love looks like at the voting polls.

Lord, we pray for our Country. But we are not afraid! *Amen and Amen.*

***

People lost friendships and respect for people as the realities of their beliefs were being revealed and exposed.

Prayer

True Friend
by
Rev. Farrell Narcisse

It is far better to receive the honest rebuke of a friend, than the insincere compliment of an enemy. True friends always desire the very best for us and are a gift from God. They love us at all times, even when we are not so lovely, and will stand with us through adversity. "A friend loved at all times, and a brother is born for adversity" (Proverbs 17:17).

***

There were tremendous efforts to get people out to the polls to vote. This election was called the fight for the soul of America.

Prayer

Voting Prayer
by
Rev. Martha Orphe

Gracious and Loving God, we are standing in the lines of life. Lord, we are standing waiting for a change to come. We are standing waiting for a better future. Lord, we are waiting in line for the healing of our nation. We are standing in line hoping beyond Hope. Lord, we are standing in line to vote.

Lord, we pray for all who are standing in line to vote.

Poem

A Letter to My Sons
by
Linda Perrodin Mallery

My great grandfather was a slave. Do you know what that means?
My grandfather was a sharecropper. Do you know what that means?
My father was a janitor. Do you know what that means?
Picture this:
You want to eat ... but you have no food
You want to work ... but no one will hire you
You want to go to school ... but there are none
You want to vote ... but you are denied that right
Sons, never forget the sacrifices that were made ...
So that you can eat
So that you can go to school
So that you can vote
Never take these freedoms for granted!

Prayer
Wednesday Prayer Call, October 13, 2020

The Voting
by
Rev. Martha Orphe

Lord God the time for the Presidential Election is quickly approaching and the tension is increasing in our divided country. Lord, we pray for safety for President Trump and Vice President Pence. We pray for the safety of Presidential Candidate Joe Biden and Vice President Candidate Kamala Harris. We pray for all the people who have been working the debates. Lord, help all to remember that the Covid-19 virus is still very active as we continue to live in this Pandemic.

Lord, we have started early voting. We pray people will wear a mask, do social distancing, and wash our hands in order that we can also be safe in this Pandemic. Lord we pray for all as we go out to cast our vote and make our voices heard. As people stand in lines let them be prepared for hours of waiting. Let us stand and wait in hope, a hope for a better future for our lives, our families, our friends, our country. Lord we know we do not all agree but help us to be people of Hope.

As believers in you O lord we pray for your Will to be done on earth as it is in Heaven. Lord we bind the Devil in the name of Jesus and we loose the joy of Jesus in your Holy Name. We call upon your name Jesus as we pray for our schools, for our children, teachers and all school workers. We call upon your name Jesus as we pray for those who are still recovering from Hurricanes, fires and other natural disasters. We call upon your name Jesus as we pray for peace where there is no peace and as we pray for justice where there is injustice.

Lord God we pray the name of Jesus for there is power in the name of Jesus. *Amen and Amen.*

***

Election Night, November 3, 2020

It was an intense night. At the end of the night, the margins were close and everybody was claiming there was a winner. Some of the country celebrated the winner, the election of Joe Biden and Kamala Harris, the first ever woman, African American, and Asian American to be elected as the vice president of the United States. Others believed President Trump was the winner, and he had won the election. Some of the country wanted to go forward with the election of Biden/Harris while others believed the continued false accusations of widespread voter fraud and stolen election rhetoric of Donald Trump and were challenging the elections with lawsuits. So we waited.

Prayer
Wednesday Prayer Call, November 4, 2020

The Morning After
by
Rev. Martha Orphe

Gracious and Loving God, you are God.
Republicans are not God.
Democrats are not God.
Independents are not God.
Non-voters are not God.
You are God and you are God all by yourself.

Lord God it is the morning after the U.S. Presidential Election. Lord, we continue to pray for this election because it is not over yet. There is no named winner yet. All the votes have not been counted yet. Lord, we pray for all poll workers, all the vote counters. Lord we know you know the results for you know all things. Lord help us to be calm as our divided country is waiting for the results. Especially for those of us who call ourselves Christians let us be faithful and a beacon of light and love as we wait for the election results. There is a saying that says, don't let the elephants and the donkeys make those of us who believe forget that we belong to the Lamb. Holy is the Lamb of God! Worthy is the Lamb of God!

Lord you know the desires of all our hearts. This group wants to name Joe Biden as president; and claim Joe Biden as president. This group wants to believe that Joe Biden will be the 46th President of the United States. But Lord there are other groups that want to name, claim and believe that Donald Trump will continue as President of the United States.

Lord God we are all praying and we all want what we want. Help us Lord to pray that thy will be done. We confess we hope your Will is our desire but help us O Lord if we truly believe that you are in control and your will is not of our likings and wants. Help us to stand in your will and in your way. Lord help us to celebrate with great joy but not be punitive and help us to accept defeat with love and kindness.

This too shall pass. Until the results are announced we will continue to live our lives in the midst of whatever may be the political climate of this country and in the midst of a Pandemic. But help us to always live in you. Amen.

***

And then we had to wait yet some more for the state of Georgia to have a runoff election in 2021 to determine who would control the Senate. We all had Georgia on our minds.

Prayer
Wednesday Prayer Call, November 11, 2020

Move Forward
by
Rev. Martha Orphe

Lord God, we have had an election and we are still waiting. Some people are tired and want to move on. Some people are struggling with the Presidential election results. Writer, Sharon Seyfarth Garner, wrote,

"God of red and blue states,
God of purple people, Hear our prayers.
Heal our way forward.
Soften our hardened hearts
Inspire us to be just
May we have eyes to see?
Ears to hear and hearts to hope

Lord, help us as a country to move on. Move forward. Amen.

Prayer

Prayer for World Peace and Comfort
by
Elaine Davis

Heavenly Father, creator of all things, I humble myself and bless your Holy Name.
I pray for love, peace, joy, and the healing of our land.
Let your Holy Spirit dwell within the hearts and minds of your people,
And give us the strength we need to make it through these difficult times.
I pray for guidance of leaders in government and help them to realize that their purpose
is to do what is right and pleasing in thy sight.

Heavenly Father, King of all Kings, help me to put my trust in you always,
And to remain steadfast in my faith as you show me the way.
Give me the wisdom and understanding to depend on your divine protection,
Because you said in your word you would never leave us nor forsake us.
Thank you for your precious Holy Spirit, who is our comforter,
And I give you praise, honor, and glory for you are truly worthy. Amen.

***

Elaine Davis and I are sorority sisters. Elaine is a hard worker and my faithful prayer partner.

Elaine Hogan Davis is a retired elementary school teacher and high school guidance counselor of the Orleans Parish School System. She dedicated thirty-six years of service to educating young people and helping them make important decisions about their academic and professional goals. Elaine has been a member of Zeta Phi Beta Sorority, Incorporated, for fifty-five years. She has served on numerous committees and in various capacities in Alpha Gamma Zeta Chapter, including corresponding secretary, custodian, and youth auxiliary advisor and is currently in her second term as first vice president. She was recognized by her chapter as Zeta of the Year in 2009 and in 2019 as Southern Region Louisiana Dove of the Year.

In addition to Elaine's involvement in various civic, church, and educational activities, she enjoys gardening, solving puzzles, cooking, and sewing.

Prayer

Be Kind
by
Rev. Farrell Narcisse

Dear Heavenly Father, I am thankful that when we come to you, we can be set free of any character traits that we do not have like you. Lord, fill me with the Holy Spirit so that I do not allow any angry words to come out of my mouth. Lord, help me not to yield to a contentious attitude nor have an argumentative spirit. May I be a kind and loving person that is a peacemaker! Help me to speak gracious things and be a good witness in all that I say and do. May I always love and do good to everyone all the days of my life. I ask this in the name of Jesus. Amen.

Prayer

Forgiveness
by
Rev. Farrell Narcisse

Dear heavenly Father, thank you for forgiving me of all of my sins and trespasses. Father, may I always be quick to forgive others for their trespasses against me. Lord, I pray that all of your children live in harmony with each other, and that we all possess a kind and forgiving disposition. Lord, give us love and understanding for each other in the family of God. Let us lift each other up when any of us fall down and may we have your virtues of grace and mercy toward each other. I ask this in the name of the Lord Jesus Christ. Amen.

Prayer

Heal Our Country
by
Rev. Robert Johnson

Our President Elect, Joe Biden spoke from this text tonight. (November 7, 2020)

"For everything there is a season, a time for every activity under heaven. A time to be born and a time to die. A time to plant and a time to harvest. A time to kill and a time to heal. A time to tear down and a time to build up" (Ecclesiastes 3:1–3)

It's a new season in America. We are not enemies; we are all Americans and better yet, Christians. Heal our country, Lord!

Reflections: Chapter 11

The months approaching the 2020 presidential election were filled with COVID-19 and political divisiveness in the United States. People were literally losing friendships, relationships, and respect for others as the realities of their beliefs were being revealed, challenged, and exposed.

1. Did you or someone you know experience such turmoil?

2. How did you deal with it? Was prayer involved?

3. Which prayers or poems speak to you? Why?

4. The massive voter registration campaign was described as the fight for the soul of America. What did you think of the elections and the aftermath?

5. People prayed (to God) for their candidate to win. How do we pray for the will of God to be done?

6. President-Elect Joe Biden declared it was a new season in America. Defeated President Donald Trump continued to declare massive voter fraud but showed no evidence. In the midst of such divisiveness, how do you think we should pray to God? How do we cover each other in prayer?

CHAPTER 12

Thanksgiving 2020

Thanksgiving was not the same. Nearly 300,000 people left an empty seat at their family's table. We continued to practice social distancing in order to prevent the spread of the virus, which was on the rise. Many in this country did not have big feasts or football watching gatherings, but others did. Throughout this holiday time, the election challenges continued, and we had to continue to pray for the nation.

Prayer

A Prayer for Our Nation
by
Pastor Robert Johnson

Lord, I come to you praying for our nation. Lord, please forgive our nation all who said nothing, did nothing, and agreed with the wrong within our leaders. Lord, hear our cry for healing and unity for the nation.

Help us to love our neighbors. Help us to care for others. Help us to care for others. Help us to look at our world through the eyes of someone who may not look like us. Help us to live our lives as examples of Christ-like people of faith. Have mercy on us. *Lord, let us realize as Americans, we are better together and we are one nation under God. Amen and Amen.*

***

But there were always reasons to be grateful.

On Saturday, November 28, my son Christopher Jamar Follins and now daughter-in-law Sheradie Ariel Jackson were married in New Orleans. We enjoyed a safe, mask-wearing, social-distancing, fun-packed, absolutely beautiful wedding.

Mr. Christopher Follins
Mrs. Sheradie Jackson Follins
New Orleans, LA
November 2020

Mr. and Mrs. Christopher and Sheradie Follins
Louisiana State Capitol Building, Baton Rouge, LA
November 2020

The Advent season began on the Christian Church Calendar. Come, Lord Jesus; shine your light into this troubled world.

Prayer

Advent Prayer
by
Rev. William B. Meekins Jr.

Ever moving, and ever present God, today we begin our journey, our pilgrimage to Bethlehem, the City of David to celebrate the birth of the Christ-child.

It's a journey that is long, and the way is tiresome and the pathway not as clear or flat as it should be.

Our spirits have become weighted down with the strain of the coronavirus and the continuing quest for social justice.

Nonetheless, we begin knowing that you will lead us into a place of hopefulness. Moving us to a place in the quietness of the night, where we find peace. In that peace where hearts are filled with joy, as you pour out your love upon and through us.

Remind us to follow the light of the star in the east where we are able to worship you with all of our giftedness and through your grace and mercy. Amen.

Prayer

Wednesday Prayer Call, December 9, 2020

A Prayer of Advent Hope
by
Rev. Martha Orphe

Lord Almighty we are still giving you thanks because every day is a day of Thanksgiving. We thank you for the beginning of yet another month in this 2020 year. Lord, many of us are glad it is the last month of the year but Lord let us remember the Season we celebrate in this month. Let us remember the Real Reason for the Season.

Lord in this Advent and Christmas Season let us see Hope. When we call on the name of Jesus there is always hope. Jesus you are our hope. You are the hope of the World.

Lord, we see signs of hope for a vaccine against the COVID-19 virus. Lord our souls rejoice! We thank you for medical science that can create a response to this virus. We thank you for hearing and answering our prayers. But remind us Lord, you are the hope of all Hope. Help us to be careful and wise about any vaccinations.

Lord, we continue to pray for the transition of leadership of this country. We in this group see some hope. Our souls are relieved. We know there is much work to be done to heal our divided nation and get things done for the betterment of we the people, all the people of the United States. We have hope in each other that better days are ahead of us. Lord, a future with Hope!!

Lord, we are looking for signs of hope. A glimpse, a sign of Hope. Shine your light that we may see you and we see others. May we see, baby Jesus, our sign of hope this coming Christmas Season. Lord Jesus, you are the hope of the world. Amen and Amen.

***

Comfort and Joy

The church was preparing for Christmas. The world was preparing for the holidays, the election challenges continued, and my family and I were brought even more much-needed comfort and joy. We celebrated the conclusion of some very special hat-wearing events: four graduations in one family in the same year, the same challenging 2020 year. They all "just did it"!

2020 grads: They just did it!

2020 Graduates

Left: Mrs. LaKeya Batiste Perrodin—LSU
Top Right: Ms. LaKaysha Batiste—LSU
Middle Right: Keyvon Batiste-St. Martinville Senior High
Lower Right: Kayvon Batiste—St. Martinville Senior High

Most graduates and their parents would express similar words of thanksgiving as this mom and dad:

2020 *Goodbye*!
This was a bittersweet year for all 4 of my children.
They didn't get to walk across that stage everyone waits for.
They worked so hard for it.
We are so proud to say all 4 graduated.
2 from LSU and 2 at St. Martinville Senior High
Way to go ya'll
Proud Parents
We love ya'll.
Continue to set goals. Sky's the limit. Hard work pays off!
Boys just finished 1st Semester of college
I won't complain. I've had my share of blessings also.
Thank You Lord!!!!
—Monica and Steve Batiste

***

They were covered by many years of prayer. Prayers were answered.

Prayer

The Road Traveled
by
Terrolyn Carter, PhD

You travel a road everyday,
Yet it does not always go your way.
It may be smooth, it may be rough,
And you always think it is oh-so tough.

You ask yourselves, "Was this the right road to take?"
"Maybe we should have gone another way.
You continue to travel despite your doubts and fears,
Never realizing, someday there will be tears

Though the road had curves and swerves, you remained on track.
Nevertheless, you thought of turning back.
Along the way, you gained three travelers one at a time.
They kept you going, you did not mind.

There are times you come to a cross in the road,
Which road to take? Left, right, front or back;
Forgot that you had three in a sack?
Remember the decision you make,
The other three, no doubt, would have to take.

All those times, it seemed like a test,
Though, your Father above knew what was best.
"Take this road and follow me, and
You will be pleased when you see
If you take my road every day,
I promise always to show you the way."

Good times, bad times, and sadness too
You wondered, if this was all done purposely for you?
Yes, it is all so true.
He wanted to make you strong like him.
So you could encounter anything.

Oh! Is this an end you see?
End of the road, no it can't be.
Another cross in the road, it seems to be.
Maybe this time you can turn back,
Now, you no longer carry three in a sack.

"Should we take separate roads and go alone, or
Should we remain together, rock solid like a stone?
The question remains to be answered by your Father,
"Take my road every day, and remember
I promised if you follow me, I'll always show you the way."

***

I love the quiet, calming spirit of Dr. Terrolyn, my sorority sister. This poem and her life encourage us to listen to God in prayer. Terrolyn is a graduate of Xavier University and received her PhD from the University of Missouri at Columbia, Missouri.

Reflection
by
Sharon Jarrett-Brown

.. Maturity is when you live your life by your commitments, not by your feelings. The difference between successful people and unsuccessful people is that successful people are willing to do what unsuccessful people don't feel like doing. They develop habits. They stay committed. How do you develop this kind of persistence? The key is to look not at your problem but at the Lord. Keep your eyes on God. "If you have faith as small as a mustard seed ..." Luke 17:6 (KJV)

A Time to Think

Have patience with all things, but chiefly have patience with yourself. Do not lose courage in considering your own imperfections but instantly set about remedying them. Every day begin the task anew. –Saint Francis de Sales

A Time to Act

Be patient, have faith and work towards what you desire.

A Time to Pray

Father, give me goals that stretch my hope to match Your might.

***

Sharon Jarrett-Brown and all the members of the 126-year-old African Women Aurora Reading Club of Pittsburgh, Pennsylvania, have been feeding my hunger and my love for reading and culture since I joined the club in 1987.

Sharon is a semiretired home-based travel agent with SURGE365. She attended Allen High School in Asheville, North Carolina (an all-girls school run by the United Methodist Church; one famous alumna is Nina Simone). She graduated from the University of Pittsburgh in Pittsburgh, Pennsylvania, where she majored in psychology. She also obtained degrees from the University of Massachusetts, Amherst, in Amherst, Massachusetts, with a MEd in administration and counseling and an MBA. She enjoys playing golf, reading, and traveling. She is widowed with one son, Carl J., and a stepdaughter, Carol Lynne.

Reflections: Chapter 12

Although the fourth Thursday in November is designated as Thanksgiving Day, many Christians believe that every day is Thanksgiving Day. In 2020, we were forced to find creative ways to be thankful. I shared some of my family blessings that were creatively celebrated in 2020: four graduations and a wedding!

1. What were some things you were thankful for in 2020?

2. And what were the creative ways that you used to celebrate your blessings?

3. Write a prayer of Thanksgiving. Make a list of songs that help you to celebrate these prayers of Thanksgiving. The book of Psalms in the Old Testament is a great place to find words of thanksgiving to be prayed to God.

Read Psalm 9:1, Psalm 95:1–3, Psalm 100:4–5, and Psalm 118:1.

CHAPTER 13

Christmas 2020

Christmas was not the same. Some gathered in groups; others chose not to. Shopping was not the same. Many shopped online to prevent the spread of the virus; some shopped in the stores. Even with a pandemic, Christmas could not be canceled. My family did Christmas in a different way. Normally, the Annual Children's Christmas in the Country would be held at my home with seventy-five or more people. In 2020, everything had changed, but thank God, everything had not stopped. The Orphe Generational Foundation (OGF) changed the in-person Christmas in the Country event to a virtual event, and now it was Christmas in the Country in a Box. Adults and children worked in the Santa Workshop.

Santa Workshop
Top Photo: Workshop helpers (*left side*) Sharika Batiste Hawkins, Shawntae Batiste
Right side: Tisha Orphe (Mrs. Claus), Monica Batiste, Ashley Orphe
Lower Photo: Brie Everett, Jaxen Blaze, and Ashley Orphe

It was a big production. The plan was for the boxes to be picked up, and children would join OGF helpers by Zoom on Sunday, December 20.

We partnered with Mrs. Wanda Porter Johnson, Justice of the Peace Ward 2, and other community leaders to offer the Community Christmas Wonderland Drive-By Parade Experience scheduled for Saturday, December 19, 2020. But because of bad weather, the event date was changed to Monday, December 21, 2020. Because of the date change, the OGF virtual event could not be held. Once again, life shifted, and we had to get creative. Even with the changes, the joint community leaders' effort made the parade a great success, and children were able to enjoy some Christmas joy.

Kids' Helpers
Brie Everrett, Jaxen Blaze

St. Martinville, Louisiana
Community Christmas Wonderland Drive-By Parade Experience 2020

Mrs. Claus (Tisha Orphe Sonnier), the Star (Wanda Porter Johnson), the Grinch (Delana Johnson), Monica Tyler Batiste, and Ashley Orphe

Christmas Eve

Prayer
Salute the Pastors

True Calling
by
Rev. Robert Johnson

After looking at many of my colleagues across the country being creative and doing worship differently during this pandemic to make sure that God's people have some type of Christmas Eve worship experience be it in-person, drive-up, sitting on the lawn, or virtual worship God used us to go on with celebrating the birth of Christ even during these challenging times in 2020.

I salute my colleagues. Some outside in the snow, some in local parks, some outside the church building, some worship services pre-recorded, some inside the sanctuary, however, we accomplished sharing the gospel. Please take some time and show your pastor and all those involved in making sure you have some type of Christmas Eve Worship experience. Pastors are working overtime during this pandemic. Give God the glory for true servants among you to proclaim the gospel.

Prayer

Christmas Evening Prayer
by
Rev. Robert Johnson

As this Christmas is coming to an end, many of our loved ones are not at the table in 2020. Many have loved ones in hospitals and thousands are fighting for their lives from COVID. Millions are not able to spend this Christmas with their loved ones just to keep each other safe.

Millions are not able to pay their rent or mortgages, not afford Christmas gifts for their children. We all have been impacted in some shape or form by this pandemic.

As I sit here thanking God for life and family and grateful to be able to see this year's Christmas, I am blessed to have the little things in life.

Before you go to sleep tonight say a prayer for all of us who have lost loved ones this year, all those out of work, all those who may be evicted from their homes due to this pandemic; all those families living on the streets, those who are contemplating suicide, contemplating drug use or alcoholism again to remove the pain.

No matter what the situation you may be facing right now, God is still good. "Rejoice in our confident hope. Be patient in trouble, and keep on praying." (Romans 12:12 NLT) *Merry Christmas to all!!*

***

The country did not do a good enough job of limiting their social gatherings. The virus continued to spread, and people continued to get sick and continued to die. I was sick for much of Christmastime, but thankfully, it was not COVID related. But, like many, I had friends with family members in the hospital with COVID-19.

My family/friends, the Browns (not Tyler Perry's Mr. Brown and Cora) of Toronto, Canada, had four family members with COVID at Christmastime. One was in the intensive care unit (ICU), and others were on a ward in the hospital. Ninety-year-old Ms. Tiny; sixty-five-year-old Luther Sr.; and thirty-something Kayode and Ness all had COVID and were in the hospital. Can you imagine not being able to see your husband, your mother-in-law, your son, and your son's girlfriend? That is enough to make some people lose their mind or lose all hope. This level of sickness can call people into yet a deeper place for the need of prayer.

When we asked Rev. Paulette Brown what we could do for them, even from another country, her words were "Pray." We covered them, like so many others, in prayer even as we watched and heard their anguish, their angst, and even their gratefulness from across the world. Besides personal calls and texts, Rev. Paulette kept us informed through Facebook:

On Christmas Day, December 25, 2020, Rev. Paulette wrote,

Waiting, hoping, praying.
Please pray for my family this Christmas

She wrote,

<blockquote style="text-align:center">
My only hope is You, Jesus.
My only hope is You!
From early in the morning till late at night,
my only hope is You."[4]
</blockquote>

What were we doing on Christmas Day? Gifts, food, football?

***

---

4.   John Paul Trimble, "My Only Hope Is You, Jesus," 1989.

The day after Christmas, that great shopping and return day, December 26, 2020, Rev. Paulette simply wrote,

Praying

She wrote of the great hymn of the church, "They are new every morning, new every morning. Great is thy faithfulness, O Lord[5]

She is talking about the mercies of God that are new every morning. They are covered by prayers and are connected to God.

Just a few days later, December 29, 2020, Rev. Paulette Brown wrote,

> Gratitude to God for all of your prayers, songs, wishes, thoughts, groans, tears and accompaniment through THE STORM
>
> "The night is gone … I'm still far from home …But the storm is passing over.[6]
> Thanks Rev. Karen for the song

Also on December 29, she wrote,

> Giving thanks and praise to God! Luther, his mother and my son Kayode all contracted COVID 19. It has been tough. God has been faithful. Thank you all for your love, prayers, and presence as we crossed a tumultuous river that looked like it would never ease up. Kayode is fine. Ms. Tiny is fine. And the newest news is that Luther left ICU just now to be on a ward. Continue healing. Prayers!!

***

Whether inside or outside the church house or in our own home, this is the moment of the great shouting and praising. Keep the faith and hope in God, and keep on moving to another day with hope!

On December 30, 2020, Rev. Paulette and I had some of the same thoughts. We were grateful—that was the message. So for the last Wednesday Zeta phone prayer call, I shared with those on the call that I was grateful and I was thankful for all of 2020. I prayed that as we were approaching the end of 2020 and the beginning of 2021, we all should be grateful. I indicated that living through this year, we were covered by prayers when we didn't know that we needed them. Gospel writer/singer Bishop Marvin Sapp sings a song that fed my soul throughout the year. This prayer song is entitled "Thank You for It All." I prayed the words of the song, which says,

> I thank you for it all
> The good, bad, the ugly great and small

---

5   5. Thomas Chisholm, "Great Is Thy Faithfulness," 1923.

6   6. Charles Tindley, "The Storm is Passing Over," 1905.

The times of victories and when I fall
I'm so grateful that I'm still standing tall
I thank you for my tears
The pain helped me overcome my fears
You been good to me down throughout the years
It's a miracle that I'm still standing here[7]

God surely brought us through it all, the good—newborn babies, building new houses, graduations, becoming debt free; the bad and the ugly—COVID-19, division, lies, violence, killings, and racism.

This song really helped me. We were still alive, safe, and well enough to gather by phone even across the miles. It was a miracle that we were still here. We needed to be grateful as we remembered the 300,000 people who lost their lives to COVID-19 and all the challenges we faced in the year.

[7] 7. Marvin Sapp, "Thank You for It All," track 1, on *Chosen*, RCA Inspiration, 2020, compact disc.

Reflections: Chapter 13

Christmas arrived and people were still getting sick and dying from COVID. We as a country did not do a good job of stopping this killer disease.

1. Where were you

   Physically?

   Emotionally?

   Spiritually?

2. Which prayers or poems or stories speak to you? Why?

3. Did you see hope? Where did you see hope?

CHAPTER 14

New Year's Eve

Day after day, month after month passed, and December 31, 2020, New Year's Eve, and the end of 2020 finally arrived. For the first time in my life that I could remember, I was not in a physical church building for the traditional Black Church Watch Night Service. Most people if they attended a service attended a virtual service even as the clock was ticking to a new year, because many of us were still staying at home to help stop the spread of the virus. I attended Watch Night Service at the Louisiana Avenue United Methodist Church in Lafayette, Louisiana, and the Midnight Cry Service of Praise, Prayer, and Testimony at Asbury / St. Matthew United Methodist Church in New Orleans, literally at the same time virtually.

Reflection

New Year's Eve
by
Rev. Clifton Conrad

I know many of us can hardly wait to put 2020 in our proverbial rear view mirror. However, we must be cautious of the message of the passenger side view mirror, which states, "OBJECTS IN THE MIRROR MAY BE CLOSER THAN THEY APPEAR!"

Moving into 2021 means putting the pains of 2020 behind us. However, when we take a sideways look at 2020, we must realize that those pains may be closer than they appear. It is going to take time for us to get over how 2020 has changed our lives. But, we serve a God who will be with us and is able to see us through whatever 2021 may have in store for us. (Read Ephesians 3: 20-21)

Creator God, as Your hand stretches open a new year, which is filled with mystery for us, help us to know that You will be with us. Grant us the courage we need to faithfully face whatever challenges we may face. We don't know what next year may hold, but we know who holds next year in their hand. Bless us, as we move into the future You have waiting for us. In the name of Jesus we pray. AMEN!

Prayer

Watch Night Prayer
by
Wanda Joseph

Abba, Father,

We your children come before your throne of mercy and grace. On this the 365th day of 2020, we thank, praise, and bless your holy, majestic, and righteous name. Through dangers seen and unseen. A Global Pandemic, Hurricane Zeta, and a Presidential Election in the U.S.A., you have kept us. You are a bridge over troubled water. Peace in a storm, a mighty battle axe. A way-out a way- in, you are the Great I am, the Alpha and Omega. You are still God and besides you there is No Other! We lift up the sick, bereaved and those who are in prison. We lift up the needs of the homeless, hungry and lonely. We plead and apply the blood of Jesus Christ upon every demon and foul spirit that would attempt to hinder our prayers, petitions, and intentions from rising to your throne of mercy and grace.

We ask for discernment as we pilgrim through this journey, for the battle is raging. Give us eyes to see and do your will, hearts that are wholly committed to you, ears that hear the midnight cry.

As we step into the year of 2021, may we throw aside every weight that has encumbered us from 2020 and before! Abba, we pray that you break every yoke of bondage, endow us with spiritual discernment to know the seasons and the voice of the One True and Living God. Let us put on the Helmet of Salvation, Sword of the Spirit, Breastplate of Righteousness, and the Shield of Faith. The Belt of Truth, as we shod our feet with the Preparation of Peace. Shore us up and make us ready for the battle. Then having done all these things; STAND.

Oh hasten the day of the Lord in the name of Jesus Christ, Son of the Living God, we ask and pray. Amen. Be Blessed Shalom

Thanking God for bringing us through the year 2020!

I missed something at Christmas. I decided to do what I would normally do for Christmas, and that was to wear my Christmas hat and outfit. I actually wore it on New Year's Day. New Year's Day was a regular gathering of food and football. I wore my Christmas hat in the middle of what would be a normal relaxing day. Even a new day in a New Year did not mean that everything from 2020 was now over. I wanted to be covered by prayers and my hat for the New Year!

Wearing my Christmas hat on New Year's Day 2021.
This is actually my mother's red hat.

I did not plan this, but notice the hat tree topper on the Christmas tree (courtesy of my sister Clara Jean Batiste). Even the Christmas tree was covered by a hat!

I don't know about you, but I like to know the end of the story. So here it is.

Happy New Year—2021

The new 2021 year began, and Rev. Paulette wrote,

> New Year's greeting Neighbors! The storm of Covid-19 hit. We are thankful for surviving. Luther came home from the hospital last night and on the path to recovery. His mom, Kayode and Ness have all made amazing recoveries. Zahra and I continue to be COVID negative, while learning how to cope with the trauma. Thanks for your love, prayers, gifts, and presence from far and near. Through you, we experienced the God who suffered with us through our trauma and who has promised that whatever the outcome may be, nothing, would separate us from God's presence and love.
>
> I'm in a different place this day—situated among the many families across the globe, visited by the wrath of COVID 19—with varying outcomes. Having walked this road, I am more convinced than ever that what's needed to support the scientific-based fight against COVID -19—hearts of justice, love and compassion to hear, see, feel and fight for the wellbeing of our neighbors.
>
> Thank you all for being our neighbors in a rough time. You've given new meaning to "Love your neighbor!" A new journey in justice and neighborly living now begins! Grateful

Grateful God brought us through 2020.
My sixtieth birthday, September 2019

If the year 2020 has taught us nothing else, I believe it taught us that our lives need to be covered by prayers day after day, month after month, and year after year, and we need to be grateful!

I hope these prayers, poems, and pictures reminded us that living through 2020 during the global COVID-19 pandemic and in the midst of racial divide and social unrest in the United States, we were indeed covered by prayer.

Reflection: Chapter 14

We survived 2020! Thank God! That major feat is not something to take lightly given that more than three hundred thousand people died from COVID-19 in 2020. One of the gospel songs that helped me in 2020 is "Thankful for It All." I am thankful for it all, the good, the bad, the ugly, and the small. This song puts it all in perspective for me. I am thankful for all who prayed for me. I am grateful I was able to cover others with my prayers to God.

1. How did you feel at the moment we rang in 2021?

2. Where were you New Year's Day 2021?

    Physically?

    Emotionally?

    Spiritually?

A Special Tribute to My Zeta Family

Poem

Haiku: Silver Sorors
by
Dr. Rosalind Hale

Five began at once.
Marching forward together.
Then they became one.

Truth each had sisters.
Siblings they would always love.
Yet each choose each other.

Words cannot explain
the bond they soon developed,
Sisterhood til death.

No words need saying.
Time never changes at all.
Five can become one.

People wonder why
they seem happy together.
It is joy they bring.

Trying mentoring
younger members as they share
true sisterly love.

Wonder what's next,
as organization grows.
Seeds planted to sprout.

For many in the United States, the beginning of 2020 was just another year. The Zeta Phi Beta Sorority, Incorporated, had started the long-awaited centennial celebration. One hundred years! In January, many gathered for the initial centennial event at Howard University in Washington, DC, where it all started. Five undergraduate women began Zeta Phi Beta Sorority, Incorporated, on January 16, 1920. Thousands of us were also scheduled to attend the Grand Boule Centennial event in Washington, DC, in the month of June. We waited over the months as we were facing the challenges of the virus. After all the years of planning, after all the waiting, the June celebration did not happen because of the COVID-19 virus. Although we did not physically gather together, we continued to celebrate our centennial because we are the seeds planted and sprouted.

The women of the Zeta Phi Beta Sorority, Incorporated, "the Mighty" Southern Region, Alpha Gamma Zeta Chapter in New Orleans, Louisiana, also began the year with a centennial celebratory spirit. And although we stopped gathering physically, we knew we would always pray for and with each other. We were physically separated but spiritually connected.

I thank God for the leadership of our chapter president, Mary Hogan Carter. She asked me, as the chaplain, to lead the chapter in prayer every Wednesday at 12:15 p.m. Several sisters from regional, national, and international levels joined on the call.

The Wednesday, June 24, of centennial week when we would have gathered in Washington, DC, some of our sorority sisters and I prayed together.

I led us in prayer:

> The hymn writer wrote and we pray,
> Be still my Soul, the Lord is on your side.
> Bear patiently the cross of grief or pain.
> Leave to your God to order and provide
> In every change, God faithful will remain.

Lord God help us to remember that we ought to leave things for you to order and provide for our lives. We may not be where we want to be, that is Washington, DC, for Centennial but we are here and we are alive. Although scattered we have gathered again to pray.

Lord, we are living in anxious, fearful, tense, stressful times. Lord God, calm our spirits for we know you are greater than any illness, disease, sickness or virus. You are greater than anything that threatens our lives but Lord we must confess to you that we are grieving, we are in pain and we are weary. Quiet and Calm our spirits as we hear that the virus continues to spread. Lord, we confess our own wrongdoings and the wrongdoings of our nation as we have contributed to the new increase in so many ways. Lord, we are bold enough to pray and ask you to eradicate this virus and heal our nation yet we do not do our part. Forgive us O Lord. Help us to do better so that together we can heal our land. Lord, we pray for racial healing and social healing from you but Lord what are we doing to bring about this healing and justice?

Lord, what do you require of us? The Old Testament Book of Micah 6:8 tells us that you require that we act justly and love mercy and walk humbly with you our God. Lord, we are trying. We confess our faults and our sins. We have treated someone badly, unjustly. We have not shown compassion and mercy even when it would not have cost us a dime. And Lord we know we have missed many steps in our walk with you especially when we have been arrogant, think we are bigger than you, or even act like you don't even matter. Forgive us O Lord, help us to do better.

But God, there are some people who are causing us grief, heartache and pain. Lord, they are not being justly by us and in fact many want to hurt, harm and kill us with their knee on our necks, noose around our necks or shoot us in the back. Lord, help us to seek justice that all who are treated unfairly will find peace and justice. In the midst of these bullying tactics, scare fear mongering tactics, Calm our Spirits.

The hymn writer continues,
Be still My Soul, your God will undertake
To guide the future as in ages past
Your hope, your confidence, let nothing shake.[8]

Lord, give us your strength, your power to stand up, engage, be the change, and make your Biblical Voice known of "thus says the Lord." Let not our hope or confidence be shaken. Show us where and how to work for justice. Help us to show compassion and mercy even to those we may think should not receive our kindness.

Lord, we pray for ourselves and we pray for others. We pray for the world. We pray for the essential workers, our churches and mosques, we pray for children at home alone while parents are working. We pray for business leaders, government leaders, Church leaders, pastors, students, protestors, police law enforcement persons.

We pray for our families and for our protection. We pray for our Blue and White Family. We pray for our Beloved Zeta Phi Beta Sorority, Incorporated. We pray for our leadership, Hollingsworth-Baker, Beasley, Bourgeois, Carter and all the sorority sisters. Continue to guide us, order us and provide for us and calm our Spirits. You have been with us 100 years, bless our next 100 years. Be still our Souls, the Lord is on our side. Amen.

As I led us in prayer each week, the prayers either began or concluded with a prayer for our sorority.

We prayed, and we prayed. We prayed during happy times, and we prayed during the difficult times. We cried, and we celebrated. We celebrated our Divine 9 Sister (AKA), Kamala Harris's announcement as Democratic candidate for vice president of the United States. We celebrated when she was elected the vice president-elect to be sworn in on Inauguration Day, January 20, 2021. We prayed for and celebrated the president-elect, Joe Biden. We will continue to pray for both of them. We celebrated the power of the vote to make a change of leadership in this country. We prayed for Stacey Abrams of Georgia and others who graduated from an HBCU (historically Black colleges and universities), defying the negativity that we must go to a PWI (private white institution) to make it in America. We celebrated each other and prayed for the work the Divine 9 Sororities and Fraternities will do to make our nation, our world, a better place.

We prayed during the difficult times. We felt like the entire year of 2020 was a difficult time. We prayed for a cure for the virus, justice, healing, school openings, and so on. We prayed for President Trump and

---

[8]   Von Schlegel, Katharina. "Be Still, My Soul." 1752.

Vice President Pence. We prayed for the families of those who lost loved ones and could not bury them like we did in the past because of the virus.

We prayed for the families of our four sorority sisters who died in 2020. For some, the pandemic prevented their families and us from celebrating their lives together. I offer this tribute in their memory:

Top photo:
Doris Pitts (*left*)
Rev. Barbara Hamilton (*right*)
Lower photo:
Jacqueline McMillian (*left*)
Soror Laurene McMillian (*right*)
Photo credit: Patricia Calvin-Scott

2020 Triumphant Sorors
Alpha Gamma Zeta
Rev. Barbara Hamilton
July 28, 1936—January 15, 2020

Jacquelyn McMillian
December 23, 1942—March 22, 2020

Laurene McMillian
April 10, 1940—April 1, 2020

Doris Pitts
February 7, 1920—December 3, 2020

Doris Pitts, at the age of one hundred years old, was blessed to see the one hundredth anniversary of Zeta Phi Beta Sorority, Incorporated.

Rev. Barbara Hamilton was a minister with me in the United Methodist Church in Louisiana.

I, like many others, thought that the wonderful sisters Jacqueline and Laurene McMillian were twins. They were not, but they were always together, especially when they had the opportunity to do service.

I thank God for their journeys with our sisterhood.

I thank God for my journey with the sisterhood. I am grateful for the support, encouragement, and inspiration we received from each other as sisters in the unprecedented year 2020. We were the seeds planted who were alive to see the one hundredth year of Zeta Phi Beta, Inc. I believe living through 2020, we were covered in prayers and hats.

In 2020, we looked forward to making some wonderful centennial memories, but that did not happen because of the virus. But we can remember our past memories in the midst of our long stay in home quarantine and new ways of living. And so I remember some of my past memories and time I shared with some sisters.

From left to right: Delecia Smith Vanzant; Mother Rosemary St. Cyr Smith; Zeta Phi Beta Sorority, Incorporated, International President Valeria Hollingsworth-Baker; Rev. Vondel Smith-Sloan; JoyVelvye B. Smith.
Insert: Rev. Martha, Delecia Smith Vanzant and Rev. Vondel Smith-Sloan

These Smith family women have enjoyed a long legacy of becoming Zeta sisters. I met Mother Rosemary Smith and her daughters while Vondel, Delicia, and I were students at Centenary College of Louisiana in Shreveport. I was there from 1977 to 1979. Our lives went in different directions, but over forty years later, Rev. Vondel and I share being clergywomen in the United Methodist Church. She is in Texas, and I am in Louisiana.

Alpha Gamma Zeta Spring 2017 intake group
From left to right: Martha Orphe, Wonda Crawford, Yolanda Walker Harris, Meleika Tyler Spencer, Janieka Mills, Tracey Powell, Betti Williams, Stephanie Dandy Cole

And over forty years later, in Spring February 2017, I became a Zeta and reconnected with the Smith family as sisters in the sisterhood.

My niece and godchild, Sharika Batiste Hawkins, had already become a Zeta in 2007. We began our family legacy at the Southern Regional Meeting in Shreveport, Louisiana, in June 2019.

Orphe Legacy
Top photo: Sharika Hawkins and Martha Orphe with Zeta Phi Beta Sorority, Incorporated, International President Valeria Hollingsworth-Baker

Lower photo: Legacy pinning Sharika Hawkins and Martha Orphe
June 2020

We would have celebrated our legacy at our 1920–2020 Centennial gathering in Washington, DC, but it did not happen because of the virus.

Joan Brown (*top*) and Carolyn Calvin *(bottom)* referred me to Zeta Phi Beta
Sorority, Incorporated, Alpha Gamma Zeta Chapter New Orleans.
Joan Brown was my spirit-guided Music Director at Williams Ross United Methodist Church, New Orleans, LA

Top photo: Mary Carter, Patricia Calvin-Scott, and Elaine Davis
Lower photo, *left to right*: Dawn Moore Collins, Lauren Brown, Cheryl Harris, Jan Dupuy, members of the Alpha Gamma Zeta No Greater Love Sisterhood Circle *Seated*, Rev. Martha Orphe

Mary Hogan Carter, president, Alpha Gamma Zeta Chapter

Elaine Davis, first vice president, Alpha Gamma Zeta Chapter

Patricia Calvin-Scott is a member of the No Greater Love Sister Circle of Alpha Gamma Zeta.

Dr. Rosalind Pijeaux Hale
International Women of Color Committee member
My mentor and my friend

Connecting with other sorority sisters, Carmelita Roberts and Veronica Benoit

Carmelita Roberts, charter member, served as president of Upsilon Upsilon Zeta Chapter Iberia Parish Louisiana for ten years. Carmelita is also the Southern Region protocol coordinator. Veronica Benoit, President, Upsilon Upsilon Zeta Iberia Parish, Louisiana.

The Upsilon Upsilon Zeta Chapter-Iberia Parish hosted a "Hats, Ties, & Praise Brunch" at my home in St. Martinville in 2018.

Forever sisters

These are just a few of the thousands of seeds that were planted and sprouted into finer women since 1920. I thank God for the Zeta Phi Beta Sorority, Inc.

My prayer: May You, O God, bless our beloved Zeta Phi Beta Sorority, Incorporated, with another one hundred years. Amen.

Reflections

We all missed some momentous events in 2020. I shared my disappointment that my sorority sisters and I were unable to get together to celebrate our one hundredth anniversary. Barring a miracle, I doubt many of us will live to see the two hundredth anniversary. With that in mind, I designed a tribute to commemorate the occasion and highlighted that although we were unable to gather as planned because of a deadly virus, we could still appreciate one another. We refused to let COVID spoil our joy!

I invite you, the reader, to design a tribute in celebration of something or someone who was living through the unprecedented year of 2020. Don't forget to share your tribute with all the wonderful people in your life!

BIBLIOGRAPHY

Chisholm, Thomas. "Great is Thy Faithfulness." 1923.

CottonTale, Peter. "Pray For Real." Track 13 on CATCH. RCM, 2020, compact disc.

Lomax, John Avery, Ruby T. Lomax, and Uncle Rich. "When the Battle's over We Shall Wear a Crown." 1940.

Norwood, Dorothy. "Somebody Prayed For Me." Track 5 on Live with the Georgia Mass Choir. MALACO, 1994. Compact disc.

Sapp, Marvin. "Thank You for It All." Track 1 Chosen. RCA Inspirations, 2020, compact disc.

Tindley, Charles. "The Storm is Passing Over." 1905.

Trimble, John Paul. "My Only Hope Is You, Jesus." 1989.

Von Schlegel, Katharina. "Be Still, My Soul."

CONTRIBUTORS

Belt, Cynthia, Rev.

Boler, Elsa

Brown, Paulette, Rev.

Carter, Mary

Carter, Terrolyn

Cole, Stephanie

Conrad, Clifton, Rev.

Crawford, Callie, Rev.

Curry, Jennie, Rev.

Cushenberry, Eleanor, Rev.

Dauterive, Kim, Dr.

Davis, Elaine

Dupuy, Janice

Edwards, Dolores

Hale, Rosalind, Dr.

Harvey, Janet

Jarrett-Brown, Sharon

Johnson, Robert, Rev.

Joseph, Wanda and Neva

Lee, Ouida, Rev.

Mallery, Linda

Meekins, William, Rev.

Moore, Darlene, Rev.

Narcisse, Farrell, Rev.

Pierre, Sonya

Scarlett, Eleanor, Rev.

Thiele, William, Rev.

Turpeau, Charity

Vasser, Beatrice

Williams, Deborah, Rev.

Winn, John, Rev.

All proceeds of the sale of this book go to the

Orphe Generational Foundation
PO Box 1081
St. Martinville, LA 70582
337-335-0615
orphegf@gmail.com

Orphe Generational Foundation is a Christian-based 501(c)3 organization created to impact the lives of people across the generations in the community through scholarship, education, and community outreach.

Lightning Source UK Ltd.
Milton Keynes UK
UKHW050647260421
382629UK00006B/61